TERRIBLE ANGEL

Surviving
the First Five Years
of Motherhood

Patricia Hart Clifford

PAULIST PRESS
New York — Mahwah

Library of Congress Cataloging-in-Publication Data

Clifford, Patricia Hart, 1944–
    Terrible angel: surviving the first five years of motherhood/by Patricia Hart Clifford.
      p. cm.
    Includes bibliographical references.
    ISBN 0-8091-3192-7
    1. Motherhood. 2. Preschool children. I. Title.
HQ759.C62   1990
306.874′3—dc20   90-40568
                                     CIP

Published by Paulist Press
997 Macarthur Boulevard
Mahwah, New Jersey 07430

Printed and bound in the
United States of America

CONTENTS

*To my mother
and
my daughter*

Acknowledgments

For their valuable comments on the developing manuscript I am grateful to Marie Faust Evitt, Carolyn Kennedy, Ann Saxton Reh, and Lora R. Smith.

I am also grateful to my husband George for financial and moral support and to my daughter Chelsea for the interruptions that reminded me why I was writing this book.

1. Terrible Angel

I pace the floor with my squalling newborn in the nocturnal promenade mothers must have taken since the beginning of the human race. This creature I hold will not listen to reason. She has been fed, burped, rocked, sung to, and cajoled, yet she howls on. Since being jarred from my brief sleep tonight, I have seen the moon travel from the window on the east side of the house to the window on the south. The moon and I are on friendly terms; I observe its progress every night and soon I may be howling too.

Before Chelsea's birth, I spent my days in the orderly world of an office where I depended on reason and logic to accomplish what I set out to do. Since her birth, I have watched the slender new moon swell like a pregnant belly and I have accomplished nothing that I have set out to do. All reason and logic have disintegrated.

I want my life back: my sleep, unstained clothes, uninterrupted meals, some worldly achievements. I want the solutions to yesterday's problems to work today, some eating or sleeping schedule that is repeatable over the course of, say, forty-eight hours. A new mother should shave her head like a nun as a sign of her renunciation of the world.

Renewed wails interrupt my thoughts. I don't think this baby likes the way I am holding her. I don't think she likes me. "I am your assigned mother," I tell her, "so you'd

1

better get used to me." She pauses for breath; I think she's listening. "I will be your mother always, even when you are old and wrinkled and I am in my grave." At this she turns purple and screams.

What if she has something serious? What if she dies because I didn't take her to the hospital? If I can't stop her crying, will someone come and take her away from me, give her to someone who will hold her the right way, someone who will know if she has a fatal illness or gas? How will I ever handle the problems of childhood if I can't do better than this with an infant?

I drop into the rocking chair and finger the straw-colored fuzz on the top of Chelsea's head, follow the dimpled folds in the skin on her legs. None of this was my doing. I was just the vessel who carried her, the laborer who pushed her from the darkness into the light. This stranger inhabited my body, now tyrannizes my nights and my days, and I had no say in the nature of her personality or her eating and sleeping whims. No sane person would put up with such total and devastating loss of control in any other field of endeavor. I have gone from being master of my own time and destiny to a warm body, a milk supply. The ground has shifted; the sky has fallen. I don't know who this tiny person is yet, and I'm not sure that I know who I am anymore.

It was only at dinner tonight that everything appeared to be in control. For a few hours I was the person I used to be. Christine and Eric, who are expecting their own baby soon, brought over a full-fledged meal, which we all ate in blissful peace while Chelsea slept cooperatively in her cradle. George and I responded to their questions about birth and infant care with the tentative assurance of our twelve days of experience, warning the expectant couple that this was the first meal we had eaten together since Chelsea's birth.

Christine and I had adjacent desks at the publishing company where we worked as editors, and she filled me in on the news of the office from which I am on maternity leave. Cheered by the tranquility of the conversation around the table and invigorated by the home-cooked food, I imagined that the worst was over, that Chelsea had finally arrived at the equilibrium the baby care books promise, and a semblance of our previous life had resumed.

Now I am paying for that chimerical fantasy, and I'm afraid that Christine and Eric have a false impression of early parenthood despite our warnings. Christine will be back at her desk in the morning, but I will be seeing the world through the sleepless haze I have grown accustomed to. Even if the promised equilibrium does materialize, I am certain that life as we knew it will never resume. People tried to warn us too, but I secretly imagined that we would find a better way to cope, that two intelligent adults could manage a tiny infant. Now there is no question about who is in charge here.

Those who write about becoming a parent all describe what happens as cataclysmic. Susan Isaacs and Marti Keller in *The Inner Parent* compare the experience to Alice falling into Wonderland. In *How To Parent* Dr. Fitzhugh Dodson calls parenthood "baptism by fire." Penelope Leach says in *Babyhood* that new parents face a "total upheaval in the pattern of their lives, their relationship with each other, the kind of partnership they have established, their expectations of each other, and their social group. . . . However carefully, lovingly, dedicatedly a birth is prepared for, it is a startling, overwhelming event." George and I prepared for the birth in

Lamaze class, but what would come after that was only a hazy blur in my mind. Now I understand that pushing the baby into the world is the only part it was possible to prepare for. The real labor is just beginning.

Adrienne Rich writes in *Of Woman Born,* "No one mentions the psychic crisis of bearing a first child, the excitation of long-buried feelings about one's own mother, the sense of confused power and powerlessness, of being taken over on the one hand and of touching new physical and psychic potentialities on the other, a heightened sensibility which can be exhilarating, bewildering, and exhausting." No one mentions all this because no one who hasn't had the experience could begin to understand it. I certainly had no idea that friends who had babies were going through such a crisis. I wish I had been more sympathetic with them instead of wondering why they couldn't get better control of the chaos and disorder in their lives.

Now the chaos and disorder are mine, not just in the disruption of a daily schedule and the physical exhaustion, but in Rich's "psychic crisis." For me, what I hear dismissed as "postpartum blues" is my reaction to the demand for a restructuring of my life, a reordering of my entire way of being. My focus on goals and accomplishments, my pursuit of comfort and pleasure have left me unprepared for the task before me.

Before Chelsea's birth, I had never in my life been so completely depended on by another person. Chelsea has emerged from the dark comfort of the womb into alien territory with only reflexes to hint at the independent actions she will one day be capable of making. Sudden movement or light makes her startle, but her entire encounter with the commotion of this world must be startling. In *The First Three Years of Life* Burton White writes, "The human newborn seems to be only partially prepared for life outside of the womb, and the first four to six weeks of life seem more like a transitional period between very different modes of existence than a time of rapid development." Now that George has gone back to work, I alone am responsible for sustaining this tiny person's life while she makes this transition and learns how to operate in her new mode of existence. It is a terrifying responsibility.

Being so completely depended on makes me feel like the father T. Berry Brazelton describes in *Infants and Mothers* who, when the doctor handed him his new baby, "sagged and grew pale." At this, Dr. Brazelton took the infant back on the grounds that this "was a bit more sudden responsibil- ity for a new young father than was necessary. . . ." I don't know any new mothers who have this luxury of being pro- tected from "sudden responsibility" when the baby is born. A generation ago my own mother did have a nurse to help with each of her three babies when she brought them home from the hospital. Even on my parents' small income, help with a newborn was an unquestioned necessity in that era of anesthetized childbirth and bottle feeding. Mine is an era of natural childbirth, breast-feeding, and hands-on parenting. I was grateful to be awake to see Chelsea emerge, and am glad I can feed her with my own milk, but I vacillate between wanting to keep this baby entirely to myself and wanting to hand her over to someone who knows something about babies.

My mother lives a few miles away and has come over during the day to help me catch up on sleep and dirty dishes. When she comes, I feel like a little girl again who wants and needs my mommy, but who also wants to do it myself and, especially, show *her* I can do it myself. Rich is right when she

names part of the crisis as "the excitation of long-buried feelings about one's own mother. . . ." The appearance of the
little girl in me at a time when I want to be in charge is
particularly unnerving. But the distasteful fact is that I have
run smack into something I cannot do myself. In the physically and emotionally weakened state following childbirth, I
can't begin to function with magically acquired skill and
confidence. I, who have spent so much of my life proving my
independence from my mother, have to admit my need for her
help now.

Acknowledging my own state of dependence and asking
for help challenges the image of the self-sufficient adult I
thought I'd become. Sleepless nights have given me an inti-
mate acquaintance with my physical limits and remind me
that will power and reason can only get me so far these days.
No amount of strength of will can suppress my needs for food
and sleep; no amount of reason can make a baby stop crying
who is determined to cry. If Chelsea is in transition between
states of being, so am I. My new state requires that I face my
human limitations every minute of the day and night. Accomplishments with which mortals try to escape this humil-
ity don't count in the Wonderland I have now entered.

This new state of being has challenged the comfortable
self-centeredness with which I have conducted my life up to
now. What I do for myself now has a larger purpose, that of
sustaining Chelsea's life. I have to get adequate sleep and
food so I will have enough milk for her and so I won't toss her
out the window in a fit of exhausted frustration. Placing my
entire being at the service of this little stranger who can only
cry and soil her diapers in return is an entirely different proposition from loving an autonomous adult who can show love
for me in return. Loving an infant requires moving ahead a

few notches in selflessness. But I am hooked; the center of my universe has shifted from my own needs to someone else's. It is a beginning.

For shattering my independent, self-centered way of being, this first child is like one of Ranier Maria Rilke's "terrible angels." She is terrible because the changes required of me mean a painful reversal of my previous direction, a conversion. She is an angel because these changes promise blessings, gifts of the spirit. I wrestle with these changes, like Jacob with his angel, far into the night. Like Jacob, I receive a new name. I am now "mother," someone I was not before. I name her, she names me, and we are inextricably bound together.

In the days when angels appeared, they never brought messages that anyone wanted to hear. They were always greeted with shock and then submission to their demands which meant a "total upheaval" in the person's life. Luke reports that Mary was "greatly troubled" when the angel Gabriel appeared to her. No one ever went out seeking angels. Angels always proclaimed, "You must change your life."

This angel requires me to change from self-sufficiency to dependence on all the help I can get, from a self-centered to a more selfless way of being, and from a reverence for reason and logic to a reverence for the unseen power that made this child whole and keeps her alive despite my ineptness and exhaustion. Polly Berrien Berends writes in *Whole Child/ Whole Parent,* ". . . the parent/child relationship exists as much for the parents' growth as for the child's." "Growth" means painful change, what the angel asks for. Her asking is loud and insistent and cannot be refused.

Chelsea's cries have now become sporadic, but whenever I try to lower her into the cradle, the howls revive. I am so tired that I am afraid I will fall asleep and drop her, so I

7

wake George who has somehow been sleeping through this racket. "It's your turn," I tell him, setting my wailing bundle on his chest and losing consciousness before he can answer.

A screech in my ear jolts me upright in bed. George has put Chelsea between us where she has slept, it appears, until the sky has turned light. Clever man. But she is hungry now, and I put her to a breast that I already think of as her property. George turns over. "She went right to sleep when you gave her to me last night. You must have been keeping her up," he grins. I curl my lip at him. At least I have the milk.

After breakfast, I take Chelsea outside for an infusion of daylight after the long night. Her eyes are open now and I turn her face upward. "Sky," I say pointing, then "tree," and I see the azure of the firmament, the amethyst leaves of the plum as if for the first time. The miracle of creation in this birth has opened my eyes to that miracle all around me. "Surely," writes Madeleine L'Engle in *The Irrational Season,* "it takes no more creative concentration to make a galaxy than a baby." A baby is as intricate and amazing as a galaxy, as all of life.

Is this what it means to give birth: to see everything new? To be reborn myself? And to feel as new and raw as a newborn must feel? Birth was as startling to me as to the one born, and now we both flounder and falter in getting the hang of what it is we are supposed to be doing with each other. We are both starting from scratch; she is trying to make sense of the world and I am trying to make sense of her.

I put my lips on the top of Chelsea's head and feel the warm pulse of her fragile life. She has taken in what she could of the galaxy, looked me boldly in the eye, and fallen asleep. Erik Erikson describes the first stage of human development in *Childhood and Society* as "basic trust." Maybe that look she gave me and her peaceful sleep are the beginning of that trust. Maybe she is beginning to believe that I will do the best for her that I can, and that together we will find our way in this enterprise ahead of us.

In order for me to find my way as "mother," I have to learn trust as well. Instead of the all-knowing, all-powerful parent I imagined I would be, I have been brought low, shown my place. The only thing I *can* do is get down on my knees and thank God for letting this baby live through the night. Maybe that is the more grown-up position after all, a surrender to the grace that has brought us safe this far.

The basic trust developed as an infant, says Erikson, becomes in the adult the capacity for faith. My original dependence on my own mother is transformed into a trust in the divine. It is maternal benevolence that I seek, the Comforter, the Consoler, the always available lap. Belief in the power of God does not depend, as I had thought, on a particular turn of the intellect which I could choose to take or not. God has seized the moment and sent a messenger; I can only reply as Mary did to her angel, "Let it be to me according to your word."

The day blazes, exulting at my capitulation; a junco trills with a clear tone. I look at the hill rising behind our house and imagine taking Chelsea up that trail one day soon. I will show her the canopies of ceanothus and the clumps of miner's lettuce she can nibble on when she has teeth.

The birth of this child has shaken me out of the sleep of my comfortable, sensible world into the pain and joy of the inexplicable. Mother and child are both born anew. The marks on my body from childbirth are like Jacob's wound in the thigh—signs of the struggle with an angel. It is a wonderful and terrifying thing to be touched by an emissary of the spirit; much is given but much is asked.

Erikson confirms that parents must develop with their children. He says it is wrong to "consider the parent as 'having' such and such a personality when the child is born and then, remaining static, impinging on a poor little thing. For this weak and changing little being moves the whole family along. Babies control and bring up their families as much as they are controlled by them; in fact, we may say that the family brings up a baby by being brought up by him."

In only twelve days I have seen how much a tiny baby can ask, yet it is only the beginning of the shake-up that will be demanded as this baby grows. The prospect of those changes is both frightening and exhilarating. M. Scott Peck writes in *The Road Less Traveled*, ". . . it would be incorrect to view the suffering and changing involved in good parenting as some kind of self-sacrifice or martyrdom; to the contrary, parents have more to gain from the process than their children. Parents who are unwilling to risk the suffering of changing and growing and learning from their children are choosing a path of senility—whether they know it or not—and their children and the world will leave them far behind."

The angels that appeared to Jacob and to Mary didn't make life easier for them, and no child has ever made life easier for her parents. In *Men and Angels* Theodora Ward says that Rilke's angels are "taskmasters rather than comforters." Basic trust, or faith, is required to follow where the angel leads through the changes ahead. With faith, I can make the struggle, knowing that when day breaks I will, like Jacob, extract the blessing.

2. Creation

Pulling the front door shut with my one free finger, I climb the steps to the driveway loaded like a Sherpa for an expedition. I lower Chelsea into her car seat, and then fill the trunk with the paraphernalia necessary for a few hours out with a six month old. To meet with a group of mothers at Christine's house I am supplied with diapers, moist wipes, teething biscuits, current favorite toys, change of clothing, blanket. baby food, and my own lunch. A backpack will hold Chelsea while I do a few errands on our way home.

Our driveway takes us down a hill past our vegetable garden, dilapidated barn, and fruit trees. When we pull onto the dirt road, I wave to our only neighbor, who is in the midst of shoeing a horse. Ed does most of his farrier work from his barn, and he and the riders who bring their horses to him provide the human population of this neighborhood. Chelsea and I travel another half mile, passing an abandoned rock quarry on the way, before we start seeing other houses.

George and I bought our country "fixer-upper" as a retreat from work and the bustle and clamor of the crowded valley that lies just over the hill. For the next six years we spent evenings and weekends fixing everything from the crumbling foundations to the leaking roof. On the day we painted the last room, we cleaned the brushes and rollers and then went to the hospital to deliver Chelsea.

Now, while I welcome the sight of green hills every day instead of office walls, for the first time I have begun to feel isolated here. I think wistfully of the cul-de-sac I grew up on with its back fence camaraderie for the mothers and block full of playmates for the children. While George and I have given up most of our former pursuits since Chelsea was born, I resist the idea of giving up this house we have so much of ourselves invested in. Living in such isolation, however, means that a great deal of my time is going to be spent in the car finding companionship for myself and playmates for Chelsea.

On our drive, Chelsea babbles merrily, as eager for the outing as I am. I reply to her chatter, by now so used to understanding baby talk that I sometimes forget she isn't speaking my language yet. She makes it clear through facial expressions, tone of voice, and body language when she is excited or surprised or uncomfortable. I sing to her and point out the sights on our way and she responds with genuine attempts at communication. Stanley Greenspan writes about this age in *First Feelings,* "Your baby is now becoming more responsive to external social interactions, whereas earlier she was more influenced by her inner physical sensations (e.g., hunger, gas bubbles). . . . When your baby is gleeful and happy and you vigorously return these emotions, the baby begins to realize that his joy can cause your joy. This link gives him a beginning sense that he can have a pleasurable impact on the world—a most important foundation for optimism and trust—and also that there is a relationship between what he does and how 'the world' responds."

This reciprocal communication certainly beats unfathomable crying spells; now it is a rare occasion when Chelsea cries and I don't know why. We are both giddy with the discovery that we can create a response in the other and every day we whoop or rant, riding together the waves of joy and despair. At last, after the frustrations of the newborn period, we *are* beginning to make sense of each other.

At Christine's house, Julie lets us in, and her baby Ryan, left lying on his blanket in unfamiliar surroundings, begins to cry. Christine is nursing Emily, who now turns her head at the commotion. Emily was born six weeks early weighing only four pounds, and Christine's life for the past three months has revolved around feeding Emily and moni-toring her weight gains. Barbara arrives with Claire, and we settle the babies on blankets spread on the floor.

It must be a heady experience for these little ones, who travel mostly among English speaking giants, to see others of their same size, making the same sounds. Meeting with other first-time mothers is pretty heady for us too; no one else is interested in the minutiae of teething, feeding, bowel move-ments, and napping schedules that we relish reporting on to each other. I didn't know Barbara or Julie until we met in Lamaze class, but relating stories of childbirth and night wakenings created an immediate bond between us. We now meet weekly and share the trials of babies' ear infections and our own breast infections as well as the triumphs of first smiles, first teeth, and first full nights of sleep.

We also share our elation at the growing relationship we are developing with these babies as well as our frustration at the all-consuming job of caring for them. Finding this com-mon ambivalence about motherhood reassures us that we are not crazy and gives us the confidence to press on. We are like the mothers Jane Lazarre describes in *The Mother Knot* who "shared the doubts and self-accusations and fears which must be frankly admitted before women who are mothers can stop racing each other to the finish line and become friends. Once the truth is spoken," she says "the women are connected to each other like men who have served together in the same army." The competition is there, to be sure; I think we all fear that our child will be the last to learn to walk or talk. But our common daily strife makes us like war buddies for whom the intensity of battle compels frank admissions.

One of these admissions is the fear that such immersion in the affairs of babies will keep us from rejoining the civilized adult world we inhabited so comfortably such a short time ago. This fear was magnified for me last month by a lunch in the park with some of my colleagues from work. While we were eating and talking, I had to nurse Chelsea and was relieved when she fell asleep so I could focus my attention on the conversation. A little while later, however, I was mortified to look down and see that I had been chatting away with a bare breast hanging out of my blouse. In my flurry to cover up I woke Chelsea into a howl that ended all possibility of further conversation and confirmed to me my complete severance from respectable society.

We mothers have a common specter of lives spent in old bathrobes, of forays out of the house always made with badges of spit-up on our clothes and crumbs of arrowroot biscuits in our hair. My tale of sitting in public with a naked breast aggravates all of our worst fears.

We talk endlessly about how to reclaim some life for ourselves, how to maintain some identity that doesn't depend on the age at which our babies start crawling or the appearance of teeth. Unlike our own mothers, we belong to a generation of women who expected to progress in our careers, who never imagined being dependent on our husbands for income. Now we are faced with figuring out how to fit our expecta-

tions with reality. We all know frazzled mothers who have
returned to work to pump their breasts during their coffee
breaks and come home every night to what Arlie Russell
Hochschild calls "the second shift" of housework and child
care. We are also keenly aware of the obstacles to finding
good child care. But the real issue centers around the relationship that is developing between us and our babies. We have
fallen in love with these wondrous beings, and despite all the
drawbacks and difficulties, we feel reluctant to turn them
over to someone else's care.

Penelope Leach explains the reasons for this. "Between
3 and 6 months people become the most vital factor in an
infant's environment and therefore in his development as a
person. He learns to know one person from another; he
chooses the person or people to whom he becomes most
closely attached, and he learns about the world through
them. He needs them to mediate the world for him, to show
him things, to help him to do what he cannot yet do alone
and to comfort and reassure him when things are strange or
difficult." We want to be the ones our babies become attached to, be the ones to help and comfort them when they
need it and to be there to introduce them to the everyday
wonders of the world. We don't want to miss out on the daily
enterprise of creation going on in their swift growth
and development and in the bonds that we are forming
with them.

At the same time, we are aware of the pitfalls of living
through our children. "You cannot affirm a child's life if
there is no corresponding affirmation of your own life and
needs," states Angela Barron McBride in *The Growth and
Development of Mothers.* For our children's sake as well as
our own we have to find a way to live that is not centered

entirely on them. In *Mothers Are People Too,* Anita Spencer writes, "Psychologists now say that giving up one's life for the sake of children is not healthy mothering. . . . A healthy mother . . . is one who is a person in her own right. . . . Her self-definition is not restricted to motherhood and her success in life is not measured by raising a 'quality child.' " Spencer says that the mother who gives her life for her child "seeks compensation through trying to become a 'perfect' mother and in the process uses her child as an indication of her success. As a result, the child acquires deep anxieties and uncertainties about his basic self-worth. . . ."

We are different people than we were before giving birth; none of us has the will to just pick up where we left off. But we don't want to end up like the mother C. S. Lewis describes in *The Great Divorce* who was kept out of heaven where her son Michael resides by her claims on his life. "I'm sure I did my best to make Michael happy," she says. "I gave up my whole life. . . ." Because she is completely defined by her son, she insists, "He is mine, do you understand? Mine, mine, mine, for ever and ever." A Spirit admonishes her, "There is no such thing as being only a mother. You exist as Michael's mother only because you first exist as God's creature. That relation is older and closer." Now we understand how easy it would be to succumb to such possessiveness, but we are each determined to find a way to exist first as the people we were created to be.

My leave is up this month at work and I have decided not to return; I will do the writing I have always wanted to do at my desk at home while my mother or George cares for Chelsea. Christine is already negotiating for free-lance editorial work and has started looking for a sitter. Barbara, an elementary school teacher, is collecting graduate school applications, and Julie, a nurse, wants to teach parent education classes. We spend the rest of our time together discussing plans and schedules, trying to figure out how to create our lives with few models of how to go about it. In *The Complete Postpartum Guide* Diane Lynch-Fraser suggests the scope of the problem, "After you emerge from that initial six-month 'twilight-zone' period of parenting, you finally realize that being a mother is a total commitment and that there is often no absolute solution to balancing your own interests and the interests of your family." There is no right or even best way to do this; we each have to stumble through the thicket, forging a path for ourselves where none existed before. At least we have company along the way.

That company serves to affirm the miraculous nature of what we are experiencing. A woman in *Mother's Talking* tries to explain why "even ninety-year-old women still talk about childbirth. . . . To have participated so directly in the creation of life and to have held that life within you . . . you don't ever, ever want to lose that feeling. . . . And every time you tell that story, you're trying to get back to the miracle." Unlike war buddies, our stories are of life, not death. We have the sense of being in on the ground floor of creation. We are what Matthew Fox describes as "co-creators," participating in the divine function.

Our babies are growing, flourishing, communicating, even tiny Emily, and this growth is evidence of a Creator at work. Playing our roles with respect for the Creator means we do not claim either the entire credit or the entire burden. Our role is more like that described by Richard Farson: "We have treated our children," he says, "as if we could shape them the way a sculptor shapes clay . . . but that's not the way it is. It's more like we are running along and we fall on a

17

pile of clay; we leave an impression all right, and that impression is distinctly us, but we have very little control of what it looks like." I need to worry less about creating the child I want and concentrate on creating my own life that will leave the impression I want to make on her.

Approaching the hills on the way home, I am struck by how their summer brown has turned green after a few November drizzles. As we head up the driveway, I explain to an uncomprehending baby how the rain has caused the grass to sprout. "In the beginning," I tell her, "God made the heavens and the earth." She begins a whimper that I know means she is ready for a nap. "Well," I say, carrying her into the house, "it's a long story, and we have plenty of time."

3. Jubilate

It is a warm June day in the vegetable garden and I am twisting sugar peas off the vines while a hose soaks carrots and radishes in one of the three raised planting beds. The fourth planting bed no longer holds vegetables but sand, and in it Chelsea is busily digging holes and filling them, making hills and leveling them. We have the appearance of harmony here, but it is an uneasy truce. I am rushing to finish the watering, picking, and weeding before Chelsea tries to confiscate the hose and pluck up seedlings before they have a chance to grow.

Chelsea turned one year old last month and has set out to master life by commandeering whatever I am using. She pushes the buttons on the phone when I am talking on it, runs off with the book I am reading, seizes my dinner fork when my head is turned. She wants what I'm eating, not her baby food; wants the pen I am writing with, not a toy. This seems to be a sensible way to learn to use the implements of our culture, but my patience often wears thin and I respond like any respectable toddler by grabbing my things back. She has started walking, and her new mobility keeps me on the defensive; I am always hurrying to finish a task before I'm assaulted.

I want to get my work done and then play, but Chelsea has not learned to make the distinction. A garden hose holds

19

endless possibilities for her; I see only its utilitarian purpose. When I do finish my chores and sit down on the floor to play with her, it never works as I envisioned. I quickly become bored with her banging blocks together and want to pile them up to make something, a finished product. Chelsea has no interest in a finished product; she needs to experiment, try things her own way. When I try to steer her in the direction of a "right" way, she loses interest and I am disappointed in my failure to play with my child.

Play is one area in which the child has to take the initia' tive; it is the means by which she explores the world. "Through play, more than any other activity, the child achieves mastery of the external world," says Bruno Bettel' heim in *A Good Enough Parent*. Chelsea goes at this neces' sary and important task of exploration with gusto, but it's hard to live with the havoc she creates. Food rarely goes directly into her mouth but must be first squeezed through the fingers or rubbed in her hair. The contents of kitchen cupboards are emptied onto the floor, then the pots and pans beaten with metal spoons. Floors are littered with toys and household objects which she then trips over in the process of navigating across the room with her unpracticed totter.

Trying to keep Chelsea from injury and the household in even rudimentary order dampens my enthusiasm for her playful experiments. Yet Bettelheim says that "a major source of self-esteem is the infant's experience that he can do things—handle objects, make them do as he desires, and make his body do things for him. . . ." This requires a good amount of freedom to explore as well as my support and encouragement despite the mess. "Only when parents give play not just respect and tolerance but also their personal interest will the child's play provide a solid basis upon which he can develop his relation to them and further to the world." If I merely tolerate Chelsea's escapades, I give her the impres-sion that her play isn't as real or valuable to her as my work is to me. However, according to Penelope Leach, "Play is not an indulgence, it is a developmental necessity: the child's job. It may not earn him money, but it earns him growth."

Sometimes I observe that growth resulting directly from play: Chelsea began crawling in order to chase our cat, and she first stood alone when she let go of the open dishwasher door to bang two spoons together. These accomplishments appeared effortless, but this child works hard at her play. She labored at putting stacking rings on and off a tapered post over the last few months, probably because I had left it alone on the floor and didn't try to show her what to do with it. Once she figured out how to fit all of the rings onto the post, she moved on to other interests. Abraham Maslow writes, "The child who is fortunate enough to grow normally and well gets satiated and *bored* with the delights that he has savored sufficiently, and *eagerly* (without pushing) goes on to higher more complex, delights as they become available to him without danger or threat."

This child has her own inner agenda, and that agenda, not her mother's, will tell her when to stop banging the blocks together and start stacking them up. I have to step back and observe what she is interested in and ready for before barging ahead with my own schemes. As soon as Chelsea could sit in a stroller, George and I began taking her on outings to places like the zoo and Marine World. Waiting in line made her cranky, and extravaganzas like the dolphin show put her to sleep. We finally admitted that the outings were more for us than for her. George and I were the ones who wanted to see the animals; at this age Chelsea prefers digging in the sand of her own yard to dolphins or hippos.

Burton White stresses the need for parents to respond to the *child's* interests. He puts in italics, "Nothing is more fundamental to solid educational development than pure, un-contaminated curiosity." The creation of a human being, it seems, involves a process of discovery, in which each step leads to the next. I have to be attentive and observant of the step Chelsea is on at the moment so that I won't contaminate her curiosity with my own impatience. Since she is changing so rapidly, the discovery process is one I have to make every day along with her.

That process is filled with surprises; this child is the wild card in my best laid plans, the joker who throws off all schedules and preconceived notions, makes two days never the same. One day in the middle of having her diaper changed on the floor, she scampered off, bare-bottomed, lead-ing me on a rollicking chase. Another day she disappeared from the first floor of our two-story house until I discovered her, grinning silently, on the landing of stairs she had just learned to climb. She will do anything for a laugh. I tell her to say "hi" into the telephone and she waves; I hand her the receiver and she holds it up to our cat's mouth. When I play the piano, she runs around with her hands covering her ears, an early critic.

I am captivated by Chelsea's antics, seduced by her hilarity, then find myself annoyed because I have let her decimate a room or usurp the time I had allotted for some-thing else. I feel as though I vacillate between indulging her and neglecting her; I can't seem to find a middle path here. Burton White warns against both extremes, saying, "A parent who routinely lets the child impose upon him or her, to the point where the baby learns again and again that his needs are more important than anyone else's, does the child no long-term favor." But on the other hand: "It is even sad- der to see a child who by two has learned that his mother is not generally an approachable human being unless she shows several obvious signs: that she is in a good mood, and that she would like him to approach." When Chelsea's needs come first for too long, I become that unapproachable mother, re- claiming my own territory. I need to draw the line earlier, not let her push me to that breaking point. An infant's needs have to come first most of the time; a one-year-old has to begin learning that others have needs as well.

Now that the weather is warm I meet with the mothers' group in the park where our children engage in parallel play, each pursuing his or her own explorations, but side by side. In the same way, Chelsea and I have to learn how to live parallel lives, pursuing our work and play alongside each other without major interference. Doing this requires some separation and detachment from the other's business, some- thing neither one of us is too good at yet. As long as I meddle in her play and she meddles in my work, we will always be at odds with each other.

I move the hose under the foliage fans of the summer squash and eye Chelsea sifting sand through her fingers. Her patient absorption contrasts with my busy scurry to get the job done. All I can see is the next thing to do; no wonder I can't sit down and play with my child. True play requires what Zen master Shunyru Suzuki calls a "beginner's mind," always "open" and "ready," with no thought of attaining something. "In the beginner's mind," he says, "there are many possibilities; in the expert's mind there are few." The "beginner's mind" is the province of every child. Chelsea can become so absorbed in sand because she is open to dis´ covering its many possibilities. For me, the "expert," the sand is merely something to keep my child busy while I get the watering done.

Annie Dillard describes in *Pilgrim at Tinker Creek* what happens to the beginner's mind we are born with. "An in´ fant who has just learned to hold his head up has a frank and forthright way of gazing about him in bewilderment. He hasn't the faintest clue where he is, and he aims to learn. In a couple of years, what he will have learned instead is how to fake it: he'll have the cocksure air of a squatter who has come to feel he owns the place. Some unwonted, taught pride di´ verts us from our original intent, which is to explore the neighborhood, view the landscape, to discover at least *where* it is that we have been so startlingly set down if we can't learn why." Exploring the neighborhood is what play is about. But instead, I've learned to fake it, to pretend that the universe is no longer a bewildering place. I can't play because I think like the "expert," who is no longer looking for the unexpected.

The vegetables are finally watered, the makings of a salad picked, and a wheelbarrow full of weeds pulled. I drag the hose out the garden gate and set it in the basin of a young apricot tree George and I planted. Distracted from her sand´ box, Chelsea follows and squats down by the tree, seizing the hose. She points the nozzle straight up, making a fountain of the water. I stick my thumb over the hose opening and make the spray reach the top of the tree. Chelsea tries this trick and squirts both of us trying to get her thumb adjusted. We put both our thumbs together, making the fountain reach higher than the small tree, giggling at the sprinkling we are getting.

Suddenly we stop our giggling, both of us awestruck by the droplets sparkling against the blue sky. Crystal threads of iridescent liquid hang suspended in an arcing cascade. Then the hose tilts a bit, changing the angle of the water, and the moment is gone. We are both wet, and the fruit trees still need watering.

Does everything look as astonishing to a child as the sparkling crystals looked to me? Is an adult destined to catch only fleeting glimpses of this world a child lives with all the time? If nothing has become ordinary for Chelsea yet, she must constantly see the extraordinary. To allow myself to play with hose water, to allow myself to be, for a moment, in a child's state of awe and wonder, is to allow myself to be surprised by grace, the unexpected appearance of the holy. "The word for the player is *surprise,*" writes Robert E. Neale in his book *In Praise of Play.* "The Holy might well be defined as the Surprising, and joyfully to anticipate and savor the Surprising is the playful response of the religious man. . . . The adult," he says, "remains on the work level for the most part and his entries into the world of play are partial. . . ." But he concludes, "What happens to the child in play can happen to the adult. And when it does, paradise is present."

If I let that spirit of play permeate everything that I do, then I could take my child's play seriously enough to let her go at it without interference. Then I could *see* the miracle of the water, the soil, the growing vegetables instead of just the next chore on my list. "True reverence," says Matthew Fox, "is more about play than it is about pious noddings of the head. For play is our response to *feeling* that we are part of a living and dynamic whole." It is this feeling that a child makes possible. One cannot give birth and not feel part of

25

that whole. One cannot watch a child play and not want to reclaim the beginner's mind that was given up with childhood.

In *Magical Child* Joseph Chilton Pearce writes that "God works and man plays—or that is the way the scheme is set up and meant to be. . . . As soon as I try to do all the work, I have tried to be God, and I mess everything up. The harder I play, the harder God works." The kind of play Pearce refers to is a way of living, not just indulgence in the leisure pursuits that often substitute in adult lives for an attitude of genuine playfulness. Neale says that these diversions from work adults call fun are often superficial means for avoiding the heights and depths of life. These "funsters," he says, "seek diversion from work, but the result is only diversion from life." A child wants immersion in life, not diversion— Chelsea is either reveling in joyous glee or wailing in tearful despair. The ability to experience joy is accompanied by an ability to experience pain, but both mean we are alive and "part of a living and dynamic whole." Fox says, "In allowing one's authentic awe and wonder to be born again and in welcoming the . . . child and playfulness . . . to come to self-expression one is already involved in co-creation. For there is no creation without play." Participating in the creation of a child requires an immersion in the process, in both the joy and the pain.

Neale writes, "Full play by the mature adult can be understood as the end goal of human development. . . . Like Moses before the burning bush, the mature player takes off his shoes and kneels on holy ground. And like David before the Ark of God, he also kicks up his heels with delight." A child seems to be born with this capacity for great wonder and great joy. Allowing her to retain as much as she can of

this spirit, her "uncontaminated curiosity," is more important than anything I might teach her. But I can only allow
her that if I participate in the mystery of the surprising, let
myself be a beginner with her. Then Chelsea will find me,
not the imposed on or the unapproachable mother, not the
expert who has nothing more to learn, but a beginner and
explorer who can kick up my heels in the hose water and
dance before the mystery of creation with joy.

4. The Fall

"Daddeeee." Two year old squeals waft into my bedroom window. They make ripples on the still pool of exhaustion where I lie, unable to hoist even my eyelids from their resting place. Father and daughter assume I am in the kitchen, soon to interrupt their play with an announcement of dinner. When they get hungry enough to look, they'll find three overbaked potatoes in the oven, tossed in with the kind of gesture of bravado that one might make before the ship sinks. Uncooked fish and salad greens wait in the refrigerator.

After flinging the potatoes in the oven, I came upstairs on some errand, forgotten immediately when I collapsed on the bed for what I told myself would be just a minute. Now I cannot move.

My mind signals for my body to get up and cook the fish, wash the lettuce, but my body won't respond. The idea of cooking dinner flickers and then goes out. The events of the day begin to unravel in my mind.

At 5:30 this morning I felt Chelsea's arms and legs scrambling over me for the center position in bed. Normally when this happens, we all just go back to sleep. But Chelsea has been diaperless at night for several weeks now, and the last time she went back to sleep with us in the early morning, our bed was soaked. So I woke up enough to tell her she had to go to the bathroom before getting in bed with us. She pulled the covers up under her chin. "I don't have to go."

I remembered the wet sheets and mattress. "You have to go."

I lifted her onto the floor and she started to whimper. George rolled over and opened his eyes. It seemed like such a simple thing. Why didn't she just go? Because I told her to, and even at 5:30 a.m. the battle of wills prevails. I put my head under the pillow. Thirty minutes more sleep, I told myself, and I could handle this smoothly.

The volume of the wails increased, and George got up and took her to the bathroom. From behind the closed door, I heard her screaming for mommy, then George's muffled coaxing. He emerged alone. She wouldn't go without mommy.

By then it was after 6:00. The sky was getting light. Two red eyes appeared over the side of the bed. "Take me to the bathroom."

Resignedly, I got up: a tactical blunder. "Carry me," she pushed for more. I picked her up by the arms, causing more howls. In the bathroom, I sat on the edge of the tub to wait.

"Pick me up and put me on."

Fed up with this game, I stalked back to bed, and Chelsea collapsed in tears on the bathroom floor. George and I stared at the ceiling, defeated.

This tantrum came earlier than usual. Normally the first tantrum of the day is over dressing. Our opinions clash about what she should wear, or I put her socks on and she has to pull them off and "do it myself." On good days I remove myself from the scene or offer unarguably clear choices. On bad days I lose my own temper and spank her out of frustration. On those days I'm horrified by my own impatience and filled with remorse.

29

I know tantrums are normal for two year olds who are establishing a sense of selfhood. Children must rebel to acquire their own identity. I just never realized what it would feel like to be the one rebelled against.

"I'm the one who carried you around in my womb for nine months," I want to shout at her. But of course that's exactly the point. Escaping that inexorable bond of the womb is a big job and requires an early start.

Having a tantrum for a two year old is like eating forbidden fruit in the Garden of Eden, disobeying the one you depend on for your life and sustenance. Like Eve, a two year old discovers that she is a separate person, with a choice. Once that realization dawns, the apple must be eaten. A baby's cry has an innocence to it; she is not being deliberately uncooperative. A two year old will cry for the purpose of sabotage; innocence has been lost.

When did she first know she could do this, I wonder. Did she lie in her crib for hours, plotting my overthrow? Or did a serpent speak to her to seize the moment? All parents notice when their children speak their first word or take their first step, but there is no place in baby books to record the first conscious act of disobedience.

After breakfast we drive to playgroup where, for working one morning a week, I can leave Chelsea two other mornings. This was my morning to supervise, with two other mothers, not just one rebel but ten. Right away, Peter and Megan wanted the same scooter. There were screams and blows. Scott's mother stepped in and struck a deal based on taking turns. I marveled at her presence of mind and made a mental note about taking turns.

Scott's mother, like most of the other participants here, has an older child. The ability of these veterans to deal with

behavior that sends novices into a frenzy is an encouraging
sign that parenting skills can be learned. These experienced
parents also display an understanding of the transient nature
of children's stages, a perspective that eludes me in the midst
of each new crisis.

This stage in which two year olds are testing the limits
of their power seems especially crisis-ridden, and supervising
ten of them for three hours is a physical and mental workout
that helped create my present state of prostration. Supervising playgroup, however, does help me to view Chelsea's rebellion as normal and gives me a chance to learn from the skill
and wisdom of seasoned parents.

For most of the morning, Chelsea defended a swing
from any usurpers; of course she ignored the craft materials I
had brought and set out on the table. At this stage when
negativism is at its peak, she is not going to make anything *I*
have in mind. "Swing away, Eve," I muttered and tried not
to feel hurt. Those who did come to the craft table didn't
actually make anything. What they did do was to sprinkle
glitter over themselves and pour glue onto the grass.

Burton White emphasizes that the benefits of a playgroup at this age are more for the parents than the children,
saying that children under thirty months old are not ready to
play together civilly. Close supervision is needed to keep
them from hurting each other as well as "repeated teaching of
civilized contact." This civilizing process takes tremendous
energy on the part of both children and parents, and by the
closing storytime we were all ready for a nap.

According to White, a child becomes ornery and stays
that way for a minimum of six or seven months because the
"young human must somehow go from a position of total
dependence and lack of self-awareness to one from which he

31

can face reality on his own (adulthood). The second half of the second year represents a stage at which a major step in this process takes place. The next comparable step seems to occur at puberty and takes the form of adolescent rebellion." Moving from dependence to independence is really what the whole ball game of childhood is about now. It is an enormous task for the child to accomplish, but it also demands tremendous skill and flexibility of the parents.

Stanley Greenspan stresses the importance of parental flexibility in helping the child make the transitions. He says that "there is nothing in the child's emotional makeup at this stage that makes belligerency inevitable; in fact, problems mostly arise from the fact that *he* is changing, and *you* are having trouble keeping pace with him. He is developing enormous new skills for conceptualizing the world, but he still feels dependent on you; he wants to experiment with powerful new feelings of curiosity or even aggression, but he still craves the warmth and security of your embrace." Keeping pace with a two year old's mercurial transmutations seems to me a humanly impossible task; the effort alone leaves me weary and spent.

On the way home from playgroup, Chelsea and I stopped in town to buy fish for dinner. Here, in the world of adults, my change of status from mother of an infant to mother of a two year old is apparent. Mothers with infants are looked at with eyes softened in reverence, the baby cooed over. Mothers with two year olds meet eyes narrowed by those who have seen the damage and heard the noise possible from a child this age.

But look, I want to plead my child's case, you should hear the songs she makes up, see the dances she does. She speaks our language now—and the funny things she says! She

32

built a hotel yesterday with her blocks, a doll asleep on each floor. And she can draw faces—she will draw yours if you ask.

Chelsea stayed close to my side, sensing that it is safe to make a scene with her parents at 5:30 a.m. but not safe to make a scene with adult strangers. She has discovered that she has the freedom to choose how she behaves. This freedom of choice she is exercising is part of our fundamental human condition. We are not dangled on puppet strings by God—or our parents. We can make choices, rebel. And we humans do rebel, on a grand scale. We have not learned how to keep even the first commandment since it was delivered to Moses thousands of years ago. Moses hadn't come down from the mountain when the people were already rebelling, making the golden calf. Chelsea is learning what it means to be human.

At home, the battle of the nap began. Chelsea has been staying awake in the afternoon lately, the time when I am desperate for a break. One afternoon I locked myself in my bedroom and, after ten minutes of ominous silence, heard the sound of running water coming from the bathroom. I burst in to find Chelsea, her clothes peeled off, proudly giving herself a bath in the sink. I was thankful that George had turned the water heater temperature down to a safe level so she wasn't scalded, but that possibility scared me into renewed realization of the unceasing nature of my responsibility for her.

Now I lie here immobilized by the weight of this responsibility. For at least the next eighteen years I am supposed to nurture this growing person who is fluctuating wildly between dependence and independence. I'm supposed to know when to give her freedom and when to exert control; to be strong myself, yet not dominate her; to teach her enough about the world so she can not only survive in it but also find meaning and purpose. And, having done all this, I am to let her go on to live her own life unfettered by a mother trying to correct her mistakes. No wonder I cannot move. My own fall from any semblance of wisdom or competence is complete.

The rabbi Harold S. Kushner writes that Adam and Eve "entered the world of the knowledge of good and evil, a more painful, more complicated world, where they would have to make difficult moral choices. Eating and working, having children and raising children would no longer be simple matters, as they are for lower animals. . . . They would have to spend their lives making choices. This is what it means to be human 'in the image of God'. It means being free to make choices instead of doing whatever our instincts would tell us to do. It means some choices are good, and others are bad, and it is our job to know the difference."

It is also our job to teach our children the difference, a job made weightier by the knowledge that children learn from how their parents act, not what they say. Erik Erikson asserts that it is the way parents lead their lives that has the greatest impact on the child, saying that in the way the development of a sense of trust in the infant depended on parental faith, "similarly the sense of autonomy is a reflection of the parents' dignity as autonomous beings. For no matter what we do in detail, the child will primarily feel what it is we live by as loving, co-operative, and firm beings. . . ." It makes me take a hard look at what I live by if that is what my daughter will reflect as she grows up.

I wake up to the smell of fish cooking downstairs. I must have dozed off. I'm grateful that the mattress didn't get wet this morning. It seems that childbirth and caring for an infant was the easy part. "Living with a child who is not yet fully reasonable and yet is chronically self-assertive," says White, "is often a rather stressful existence." Stressful, but essential. If humans didn't have freedom to make choices, we would be like animals whose instinctual actions have no meaning. I can't make Chelsea's choices for her all her life, so she has to start practicing making some herself. That way she can find out what consequences her choices have. Right now I can be there to make sure she doesn't hurt herself or anyone else too badly. I have to hope that somewhere in this process she will develop the ability to make good choices when she is grown.

David Elkind talks in *The Hurried Child* about the "freedom-responsibility contract" that is "fundamental in all parenting. . . . Parents," he says, ". . . expect that as children grow they will progressively be able to take responsibility for their own behavior. But the parents must sensitively monitor the child's level of intellectual, social, and emotional development in order to provide the appropriate freedoms and opportunities for the exercise of responsibility. Consequently, as children mature, the freedom-responsibility contract is rewritten again and again. . . . Contractual violations . . . occur when parents do not reward responsibility with freedom or when children demand freedom without demonstrating responsibility." Fine-tuning the contract for a particular child on a particular day takes acumen that probably improves by the time the next child arrives. How well I can manage to keep the freedom-responsibility contract current during those years will probably determine the severity of the adolescent rebellion. I have to keep in mind that the ultimate goal is autonomy and be willing to grant the freedom when Chelsea is ready for the responsibility.

M. Scott Peck says that the root of all the problems that

patients come to psychiatrists for is some failure to accept responsibility for their problems and their lives. He says that "if they are to be healed, they must learn that the entirety of one's adult life is a series of personal choices, decisions. If they can accept this totally, then they become free people. To the extent that they do not accept this they will forever feel themselves victims." Chelsea has to learn to carry the weight of her own freedom, the burden and gift of every human being since Eve. It is the major lesson of a long childhood, and how well she learns it will determine how well she can function as an adult.

My arms and legs can move now and I propel my body down the stairs, back to the sometimes overwhelming responsibility of motherhood. Chelsea greets me shouting, "Dinner! Dinner!" George is taking the fish out of the pan and Chelsea shows me her newly acquired skill at tossing salad greens. I hug them both and George asks me if I feel all right.

"I feel better now," I tell him. "Thanks for letting me sleep."

"Mommy nap," Chelsea says.

"Yes, mommy was taking a nap," I tell her. "Mommy was very tired."

5. Incarnation

George, Chelsea, and I perch motionless on the edge of the bed waiting for a fox who comes for the fruit of our mulberry tree. We face the window that frames the top of that tree, invisible to us now in the moonless darkness. The tree comes out of a hole in the roof of the entry porch because we couldn't bear to cut the tree down when we built the porch. We have been rewarded with the sight of cedar waxwings eating the mulberries, and now this fox. Two nights ago George and I were drifting into sleep when we heard scuf-fling noises on the porch roof. Switching on the outdoor light, we saw a small creature gobbling the berries that had fallen onto the roof. Last night he returned, again undis-turbed by the light we flicked on when we heard him arrive.

Tonight we are allowing Chelsea to stay up past her bedtime for the event. Her respect for this honor is reflected in her transfixed immobility: I have never seen her hold still for this long. Sitting so quietly with Chelsea and George in the darkness, I feel the pull of the invisible tether that binds the three of us. We now constitute a family, what Therese Benedek describes in *Parenthood* as "a closely knit organism thriving on a delicate balance of its emotional currents." The interaction of these currents means we are each changing as well as being changed by the others.

George and I are certainly not the same people we were

37

before Chelsea's arrival. If I am now "mommy," he has be-come "daddy," and the weight of those names has had a drastic impact on our relationship. Having a child created an irrevocable bond between us: no matter what happens, we will always be Chelsea's parents. This bond was forged in the preparations during pregnancy, the ordeal of labor and birth, the shared wonder at the growth of tiny hands and feet, and the shared fears over high fever in the night.

But if the ties between us have been solidified, they have also been strained by the intervention of a third party into the already challenging proposition of living as a couple. Time to be alone together has become a rare commodity, and without it our relationship falls into disrepair. The fact that George has become the designated wage earner and I have become the designated parent has shifted the equality of the partnership we once had and created a new source of strain between us.

"Designated parent" means that I am the one who can't walk out the door or work at my desk without arranging for Chelsea's care. It also means that when George and I are both reading the newspaper, I am the one Chelsea will choose to talk to because she is used to me interrupting what I'm doing to respond. Now that she is talking fluently, her constant patter demands an attentive listener, and when I am serving this role for a good part of the day, I want George to take over in the evening. This need of a two and a half year old to use and master the language is even more consuming than the physical needs of an infant because it takes over my mind, pushing out any thoughts I might have of my own.

As parents of a first child, George and I expect a lot of ourselves and each other, want to do things the "right" way, and so we argue about whose way is "right." My responsibility for Chelsea gives me the edge of authority on her current favorite food, toys, and stories, and I use this edge to demand that George do things my way. When he defers to my author-ity, I get angry at him for not being more involved in Chel-sea's care.

We all make unreasonable demands on each other; it is a novel sensation to be sitting here in silence together with no one asking anything of anyone else. Our explicit demands only hint at the more implicit expectations we have for our life together. "The little child," says Irene Claremont de Castillejo in *Knowing Woman,* "projects the unconscious in all its power for good and evil on its mother. It projects the wisdom of the ages on its father, and they in turn project their future, their ambition and their immortality on their child." No wonder we spend so much time angry and disap-pointed at each other; none of us can begin to be what the others want us to be. George and I can try to sort out the reasonable demands from the unreasonable, but Chelsea is too young and too trusting of us to know the difference. We want her to be adorable, precocious, and perpetually good-na-tured, to be the fulfillment of our unrealized possibilities without our faults and weaknesses. Angela Barron McBride writes, "You look toward the child to confirm your virtues—real and imagined—and in seeing yourself in miniature, you hope to find proof of your basic lovability."

Such impossible expectations signify a major change from the days when families were depending on each other only for physical survival, as Bruno Bettelheim points out. "Since the unity of the American family, if not in large mea-sure its *raison d'être,* now rests on the emotional ties of its members to one another, they make much greater emotional demands of one another; they also have much higher psychological expectations of the satisfactions with which family living ought to provide them. It is these much greater, while at the same time much less tangible, demands and expectations that make family relations so precarious. . . ." We now ask nothing less than happiness and fulfillment from each other, things that are impossible to provide for someone else.

What seems more realistic to work toward is learning how to give and receive the emotional support that we all need to grow and thrive, a need that is genuine and reasonable. If we can make a stab at this, maybe our unreasonable demands will diminish. Only parents can give to their children emotional warmth and well-being, self-respect and a feeling of worthwhileness says Bettelheim, "and they can do so best when they also give them to each other." This is what we are about as a couple and a family. The strain of having a child has thrown us off, into criticism and resentment, which undermine the emotional security we need from each other. The initial delirium of having a new baby, like the infatuation of new romantic attraction, has worn thin, and we are now faced with the labor of learning to live together so that each person benefits from being part of the whole.

Virginia Satir writes in *Peoplemaking,* "What often happens is that the pressure of parenting gets so overwhelming that very little of the self of either parent finds expression, and the marital relationship grows weak with neglect. At this point many couples break up, give up, and run away. . . . Unless the marital relationship is protected and given a chance to flower and unless each individual in the partnership has his own chance for development, the family system becomes crooked, and the children are bound to be lopsided in their growth." George and I have to balance Chelsea's needs with our own, as individuals and as a couple, a trick that requires the proficiency of a high wire artist.

It is clear to me, however, that a child of this age can be taught to respect the needs of her parents. One day I was sitting at my desk, casually rearranging some papers, when Chelsea came in and insisted that the door to the room be closed. She has learned that when I work at my desk, the door of the room is closed, and I am not to be interrupted. I couldn't tell her that it was all right for the door to be open and for her to come in on this day without destroying the clarity of the limits she has learned already to observe.

My eyes are now adjusted to the darkness and I can make out the resemblance between George and Chelsea in the slope of the forehead, the shape of the chin. Her likeness to both of us is a constant reminder of how much a part of us she is. Such bonds make it difficult for us to disentangle our projections and allow ourselves and each other to be the individuals we were created to be. Bettelheim describes this conflict inherent in a family between the needs of the individual and the needs of the group: "Once it became accepted that each individual should not only be permitted but had an obligation to be truly himself, to develop his personality as he wished . . . tensions among the members of a family increased. . . . This, then, is the paradox: although solidarity of the family alone makes individuation emotionally safe, personal uniqueness tends to define itself in contrast to others—mainly in contrast to those we know best—and this is disruptive to social harmony."

This conflict can result in any of us suppressing our own development to minimize disruption of the family unit, which may mean placid surface waters hiding frothing re-

41

sentment and rage underneath. If Chelsea sacrifices her uniqueness to try to live up to our projected expectations of her, if George or I perceive that we have sacrificed too much of our life as a couple or as individuals to raise a child, then we are all slowly eating each other alive and the family must die along with the individuals in it.

How can the conflict between the needs of the self and the needs of the family be reconciled so that we don't all have to become hermits to avoid the sacrifices involved in living together? How can we find love among all these snares of family life? "It is true that love involves a change in the self," says M. Scott Peck, "but this is an extension of the self rather than a sacrifice of the self . . . genuine love is a self-replenishing activity . . . it enlarges rather than diminishes the self; it fills the self rather than depleting it." Genuine love doesn't demand sacrifices greater than it is humanly possible to make. Genuine love allows family solidarity to be built on the personal uniqueness of each of us.

A soft thud outside makes all of us jump. George silently flicks on the light. The closeness of the grey-brown fur to the window startles us, but the fox is too occupied snuffling up the mulberries that have fallen during the day to look up. When the light went on, Chelsea moved only her eyes, which widened to take in the pointed nose, the plume of a tail. But now she can't hold still another second and rushes over to press her face against the window. The fox looks up, and, still chewing, stares directly at her. Then he swallows and sniffs for another berry. I let out my breath. Either this creature can't see that well into the dark room or he is too greedy to care.

Only after he has scoured every inch of that roof does the fox vault onto the driveway and out of our sight. I dash to another window to try and see where his nightly rounds take him next, but he has vanished. Silent for so long, Chelsea now exuberantly recounts what she has seen. But her eyelids soon begin to droop, and George carries her into her bed. Together, George and I stand outside her door eavesdropping on her fading chatter and waiting for her to fall asleep.

Parents, it seems, are always waiting: for the child to be born, to sleep through the night, to learn to walk and talk, to get out of diapers. "Nothing worthwhile in life is sudden," writes Anthony Padovano in *Dawn Without Darkness*. "We wait for birth. We wait for life to reveal its meaning, year by year, experience by experience. Waiting is the law of life, the measure of love. . . . Birth happens to those who have waited in the darkness. Life goes on, as we know, in this darkness. Once darkness is touched by the presence of life, it grows toward the light. And light dawns unfailingly."

Only once before in her life have I seen Chelsea in the state of quiet awe she was in tonight while waiting for the fox. It was during the weeks before Christmas when we lit the candles on the Advent wreath each night. Lighting the Advent candles signifies a waiting and, like waiting for the fox, brought us together in wonder toward something beyond ourselves. In Advent we re-enact light coming into the darkness as a reminder of God's presence in the world. Turning toward that presence brings us together by revealing our common bond in the holy. Martin Buber writes in *I and Thou*, "Extended, the lines of relationships intersect in the eternal You." Perhaps we need to recognize this spiritual nature of our connectedness before we can relax our demands and allow each other our own identities.

Mostly, we struggle in darkness, trying to love each other, trying to be ourselves yet meet each other's needs. We fail a lot, especially at love; at times it seems that George and I barely have the resources to be civil with each other much less provide the emotional support that is so critical for Chelsea's growth but that we parents need as well. Then it seems that the light will never dawn, that the love heralded by Christmas will never come.

However, the possibility of love is always present. "Love happens," says de Castillejo. "It is a miracle that happens by grace. We have no control over it. . . . It comes, it lights our lives, and very often it departs. We can never make it happen nor make it stay. . . . Where love is, it is as though some presence had alighted, a third, a something else, a something greater than the little persons who are involved." Love takes us by surprise, like the fox. But we can encourage its presence and wait in expectation for its arrival. "To me it is man's task, his greatest task, not to learn to love, but to learn how to create the conditions in which love can alight upon us and can remain with us," de Castillejo writes. Moment by moment, we are learning how to create the conditions necessary for love. Every time we discern and respond to a genuine need in the other, every time we empathize instead of criticize, we are tilling the soil for the fragile sprouts of love. Before the sprouts appear in the light, the seeds have to lie in the darkness. The conditions of love are formed in that darkness, in the balance each of us has to cultivate between our own needs and the needs of the family.

In Advent we sing, "O come, O come, Emmanuel. . . ." But Emmanuel, God-with-us, has come as surely as there are foxes living in the hills. When the light appears we see what has been there all the time and then we call it a miracle. "It is solely by virtue of his power to relate that man is able to live in the spirit," writes Buber. Without each other we could not know the "eternal You." With this in mind, we can do the work of cultivation and watch and wait together for the incarnation of love to grow in each of us. Then when we catch a glimpse of love sprouting, we can call it a miracle.

6. The Questions of Job

For three years now I have carried Chelsea for any distance away from home by front pack, back pack, piggyback or stroller. Today we are setting out on the trail behind our house for the top of the mountain and Chelsea is on her own two feet. My backpack is light with only food and a water bottle, and my heart is light at the prospect of walking with my daughter as a companion.

Chelsea's exuberance is revealed in her erratic gait— she'll stop for a while to examine a rock then sprint ahead around a bend so she can jump out and scare me. This is a far cry from the steady stride with which I hiked here before she was born. Then I was escaping life's harried pace in the serenity of the wooded trail and in the sweeping vistas of the summit. Chelsea has no harried pace yet, nothing to escape from. She is not interested in the landscape or the vistas but only in what is tangible, or "do-able," as she puts it: gathering twigs or munching on the miner's lettuce from the side of the trail.

I am hoping that all this activity doesn't consume her energy before we are halfway to the top, but then I am the one who is more often physically exhausted by trying to keep up with her. Now that she has reached three and started asking "why," I am often mentally exhausted as well. Nothing that she encounters goes unexplored, unquestioned. Already on this hike she has noticed an animal's burrow I never saw before and asked if a rabbit or a fox lives there. I am hazy on the facts here, but she settles for the speculation I provide. I wonder how much longer she will settle for my speculation on questions I don't have answers for.

We are at last walking side by side when we round the next bend and almost stumble on the mauled, bloody carcass of a fawn in the middle of the trail. Dogs must have attacked it or maybe a coyote. I want to hurry around it, but Chelsea refuses to budge until her curiosity about this grizzly sight is satisfied.

She bends down and peers into the fawn's glazed eyes. "Does it hurt?" is her first question. I cringe and shake my head, wondering how much terror and pain the fawn suffered before it died. Chelsea persists: "Why did it die?" I always planned on dealing with disconcerting questions with equanimity and reassuring wisdom, but my stomach is queasy from the sight of the bloody flesh, and her questions only breed mine: Why do the innocent suffer and die?

For many years a bull lived on the grassy hillside next to our house. One day last month the bull finally became too old to stand up and someone had to come and shoot him. From our window, Chelsea and I watched his burial (with a bulldozer!) in the very spot in the pasture where he had spent most of his days. It seemed to be a fitting end to a good and long life, but everything about this fawn's death seems unfitting. Such violence to the fawn's young body clashes with my sentimental desire for a benign, just universe.

Chelsea, like all children, is a hard core realist with no interest in sentiment. If I had seen the fawn first, I would have turned back and taken a cutoff to avoid it. Chelsea forces me to confront what I wouldn't have looked at without her, asks the questions for which I have no answers. My instinct is to protect Chelsea (and myself) from life's nastiness. But to her the fawn's death is evidence in the mystery of an existence she is trying to figure out.

Right now, the book Chelsea asks to be read repeatedly is *The Story of Babar,* which begins with the shooting of the elephant's mother. At Easter, Chelsea's Sunday School emphasizes eggs and bunnies as the symbols of resurrection, but she wants to know what it feels like to be crucified and what happened to the body in the tomb. When she peers over my shoulder while I am reading the newspaper, Chelsea goes right for the carnage, asking, "Why are those people lying there? Are they alive?" I grumble at the newspaper for showing so graphically the results of accidents, murder, and war, and vow to turn the page faster the next time I hear her coming.

But turning the page or avoiding the fawn will not change what has happened and will continue to happen as long as we inhabit the earth. Chelsea's questions are not idle conversation. She has a stake in finding out how things operate in this world. Set down on this planet, she is compelled to learn our customs, rules, and habits. Her questions about the fawn and about the pictures in the newspaper have the same urgency. She is driven to discover what goes on here.

What Chelsea understands about death, I'm not sure. She can say that the fawn has died, but she has not yet experienced the permanence of loss with a pet—or someone she knows. Elisabeth Kübler-Ross says in her book *On Children and Death,* "Very young children have no fear of death. . . . Later on children are naturally afraid of separation. . . . When children reach age three or four, in addition to the fear of separation comes a fear of mutilation. This is when they begin to see death in their environment. They may see a car run over a cat or a dog and associate death with a mutilated, horrible body. . . . After about age eight or nine, children, like grown-ups, recognize the permanence of death." This encounter then is a normal part of the development of a child's understanding, but I am shaken by this necessary loss of innocence.

I take Chelsea's hand and stride off, leaving most of her questions unanswered, but it's no use trying to hand out canned wisdom for her comfort; I am the one who wants comfort—or at least a sensible explanation for the questions that have been raised in my own mind by this sight. Why are we created to love each other—and then forced to leave each other in death? It seems to be a cruel trick, this pain of human loss, which seems to transcend all other forms of human pain.

Chelsea scampers ahead under canopies of purple ceanothus. After a couple of rest stops for water and M&Ms, we do at last reach the very top of the ridge where I collapse in a field dappled with lupine and poppies. Chelsea, incredibly, still has energy to race the breeze through the swaying grass. For her, even the summit is "do-able." For me, the encounter with the fawn has left me limp, disconcerted.

Ernest Becker in *The Denial of Death* describes the problem: "Man is literally split in two: he has an awareness of his own splendid uniqueness in that he sticks out of nature with a towering majesty, and yet he goes back into the ground a few feet in order blindly and dumbly to rot and disappear forever. It is a terrifying dilemma to be in and to have to live with." If I haven't begun to acknowledge this fundamental human dilemma myself, how can I begin to explain it to my child?

When I was growing up, my parents subscribed to the

then-current wisdom that children were supposed to be protected from the disagreeable aspects of reality. And so I grew
up believing death and illness to be aberrations in what
should be a painless existence. Whenever one of my grandparents died, I had the impression that something had gone
wrong, something too awful to talk about. I never saw either
of my parents cry at those times, nor did they talk to my
sisters and me about how they felt about losing their parents.
The ultimate effect on me was the same as if my grandparents
had moved away; I just didn't see them anymore. I never
learned to view death as a permanent separation that was a
natural and inevitable part of life. I never learned that griev-
ing for this separation was the human thing to do. My parents believed that carrying on with life, at least in front of the
children, was the proper behavior, and so my sisters and I
swallowed our sadness and our questions and carried on.

This attitude remains pervasive in our society, according to Stephen Levine in *Who Dies?* "We live in a society
conditioned to deny death," he says, and cites the exorbitant
expenditures of time and money we make on keeping away
the signs of aging that indicate death's inevitability. Children
haven't yet learned this conspiracy of concealment and em-
barrass parents by blurting out the truth about wrinkled skin
and gray hairs. Yet these symptoms expose an undeniable
reality they have a right to know about.

I shrink from talking to Chelsea about what I have been
accustomed to denying myself. Yet it is her innocent insis-
tence on the truth that brings my denial out in the open. My
parents' denial of death was unspoken and unconscious, but
once I am conscious of the grief that I have swallowed and
the lost opportunities to comfort and be comforted, I can no
longer be silent. If I want Chelsea to grow up fully participat-

ing in life, then I can't limit my own participation to its painless aspects. "Healthy children will not fear life," says Erik Erikson, "if their elders have integrity enough not to fear death."

It requires integrity to admit mortality to a child who is developing trust in the dependability of her parents. Acknowledging my powerlessness in the face of death means being demoted from the parent who possesses all knowledge and has the power to make any hurt better with a kiss. The truth is that no one really knows what happens after death or why some people live to old age and some die young. I don't want to offer Chelsea the easy optimism that everything happens for the best even though we don't know why. Even worse is to say that suffering and death is God's will, making her blame God for human pain. Instead, I have to admit to her the enormity of the mysteries of our existence.

One night, George, Chelsea and I camped out under the night sky on a mountaintop in a place like this. While we watched the light turn to darkness and the stars appear, Chelsea asked the questions that people have asked from the beginning of time about how it is that we came to be on this planet floating around in such unfathomable blackness. George and I tried to explain what we knew, but we were finally silenced by the vastness of our ignorance about what we are doing on this particular planet in this particular universe, not even knowing for sure if there is anyone like us somewhere out there.

In *The Medusa and the Snail* the biologist Lewis Thomas concludes, "We are ignorant about how we work, about where we fit in, and most of all about the enormous, imponderable system of life in which we are embedded as working parts. We do not really understand nature, at all. We have come a long way indeed, but just enough to become conscious of our ignorance. . . . Only two centuries ago we could explain everything about everything, out of pure reason, and now most of that elaborate and harmonious structure has come apart before our eyes. We are *dumb*." When Chelsea enters the educational system, I suppose the aim is for her to come out with an understanding of the depths of our ignorance. She should come out asking questions, the same kinds of questions she is asking now, and she will learn what attempts have been made on the summit and where they have succeeded or failed.

Then she will be left, like Job, to arguing with God, demanding explanations, justice. A parent, trying to explain the unexplainable, can succumb to the trap of Job's friends who made his suffering worse with their wellmeaning speculation on the situation. Carl Jung declares in his *Answer to Job* that the moralizing of these friends denied Job "even the last comfort of sympathetic participation and human understanding. . . ." If rational, scientific, or even theological explanations can't answer the ultimate questions about suffering and death, at least we can comfort each other in the face of our ignorance. Rabbi Harold S. Kushner says, "Job asked questions about God, but he did not need lessons in theology. He needed sympathy and compassion and the reassurance that he was a good person and a cherished friend."

Bruno Bettelheim asserts in *The Uses of Enchantment* that fairy tales convey the same message to children. The ending, " 'And they lived happily ever after'—does not for a moment fool the child . . ." he says. "But it does indicate that which alone can take the sting out of the narrow limits of our time on this earth: forming a truly satisfying bond to another.

The tales teach that when one has done this, one has reached the ultimate in emotional security of existence and perma‐ nence of relation available to man; and this alone can dissipate the fear of death."

All children as they grow have to give up the notion of their parents as all‐knowing and all‐powerful. To fill the chasm of insecurity that is left, parents have to let them know that we will not withdraw in the face of life's unanswerable questions but suffer with them in the pain that mortal life brings. As children have to give up their notions of omni‐ scient, omnipotent parents, so do adults have to give up their notion of a magical God who will provide a reason for every tragedy and fix what is broken if we say the right prayers. What fills the chasm left by the absence of this magician is the suffering God of the cross, whom Jung calls the "answer to Job." Finding a God who suffers with us instead of making things turn out the way we want can be as much of a disap‐ pointment for the adult as the child finding her parents to be fallible and vulnerable beings. Yet parents have to accept the comfort of that suffering God themselves if they are to fulfill their task of transmitting God's love to their children.

Kushner addresses the questions of human suffering and death and concludes, "In the final analysis the question of why bad things happen to good people translates itself into some very different questions, no longer asking why some‐ thing happened, but asking how we will respond, what we intend to do now that it has happened." At the basis of our response is our answer to Kushner's question, "Can you learn to love and forgive God despite His limitations, as Job does, and as you once learned to forgive and love your parents even though they were not as wise, as strong, or as perfect as you

needed them to be?" Because "the ability to forgive and the
ability to love are the weapons God has given us to enable us
to live fully, bravely, and meaningfully in this less-than-per-
fect world. . . ."

I can't respond to death by pretending that it doesn't
exist, not when it appears, as it will, in my path. Can I let
myself grieve at loss? Can I offer comfort and let myself be
comforted? Can I have the courage to live life fully knowing
that I and those I love will die eventually, and possibly even
tomorrow? Making life "do-able" means jumping in, risking
getting hurt, embracing the natural phenomena of both birth
and death as much as I embrace this hilltop and these wild-
flowers. In *Mothers Talking* a father whose twenty-one
month old son died said, "People talk about this as being so
extraordinary. But death isn't extraordinary. What is extraordinary is the life that has been given us."

Ignace Lepp writes in *Death and Its Mysteries,* "It is my
conviction that an intense love of life is the best and perhaps
the only effective antidote against the fear of death. There is
no need to repress fear or forget that we are mortal. But we
can realize that we might die at any moment and yet live as
though we were never going to die. . . . It is precisely the
great lovers of life who encounter death with serenity and, in
many cases, with joy." As for the eternal nature of the soul,
Lepp says, "the more authentic we are as persons and the
more spiritually alive we are, the more immortality will seem
to us as one of those basic truths that need no rational proof."

I follow Chelsea down the hill the way we came, past
the fawn, not insisting on the shortcut. I try to address her
present concerns, telling her that the animal that attacked the
deer was following its instinct and that the same animal is

afraid of humans and won't attack us. I say that the fawn was surely frightened and in pain but is not hurting now. She seems satisfied for the moment, and leaving the fawn behind, darts ahead of me down the trail, eagerly anticipating whatever might appear in her path.

7. Transfiguration

I am sprinting from the car to the house when I am stopped in my tracks by something in the air. A faint breeze rustles the tall grass on the hillside, now faded to a pale straw, and what I catch is the scent of fall. I have just delivered Chelsea to her new preschool and I'm in a hurry to get to my desk for a few precious uninterrupted hours of work. But the fragrance of vanishing summer entices me down the hill to sit in the tall grass for one last time this year. This afternoon a man with a tractor will come to disk this hillside, leaving bare earth ready to produce new shoots when the winter rains come.

From my spot in the grass I can see amber splashes of poison oak and the bare branches of the buckeyes across the canyon. Chelsea began preschool two weeks ago, and I have been so intent on taking advantage of the time she is away that I haven't noticed the seasons shifting around me.

I bustle Chelsea out the door three days a week now, and she is eager to go. She adores playing with this group of children her age; adores the games, songs, and stories, as well as the chance to paint, swing, and climb. I relish the regular mornings I now have for work and am easily annoyed at any dawdling that threatens to cut into that time. This subjec-tion of mine to the clock must mystify Chelsea; like all three year olds, she is free from adult bondage to the dictates of chronological time.

Being born onto this earth and having to adjust to its temporal ways must be for a child like shifting through cosmic time zones. Maybe that's why so many books children love are about abandoning earth time for another dimension, one that is more familiar to them. I need to live with more awareness of that other dimension instead of trying to rush Chelsea into forgetting about it, which she will soon enough, just as the children in Mary Poppins forgot how to understand the language of the birds. I keep close watch on the clock and the calendar and in doing so risk missing the fragrance of fall and the very existence of birds.

Lingering in the grass brings me into the spirit of the present moment, and, still in this spirit when Chelsea returns from preschool, I agree to play dress-up with her. Dress-up is one of Chelsea's favorite activities these days, and when she concocts an outfit out of old clothes I put into a trunk for that purpose, she can always count on me for a genuinely astonished reaction. Before today, however, I haven't capitulated to her frequent requests to see me in a costume. Now I put on George's cowboy boots, a leather vest, string tie, and the closest thing I can find to a cowboy hat. Chelsea, who tends to favor lace and sequins, takes off my hat, hands me a ballerina's tiara from her last Halloween costume, and replaces the cowboy boots with high heels. I fashion a cape from a sheet, add some sparkling earrings, and receive her approval.

There is something about a costume that shakes me out of my carefully constructed adult persona. When I was a child, the roles I imagined myself in were limitless: cowboy or fairy princess, gypsy or train engineer. As I grew up, choices were made, possibilities eliminated. In playing at dress-up, the possibilities return. This child, with all her life before her, makes me remember what it felt like when I entertained the notion of growing up to be a snake charmer.

Chelsea blissfully rummages through the trunk, trying on the most outlandish combinations of clothing she can find. This stage, according to Erik Erikson, is characterized by the child's growing conviction that "I am what I imagine I will be." Once the child has gained a sense of autonomy in his twos, he "must now find out what kind of a person he may become." Erikson says that the development of both language and locomotion permits the child "to expand his imagination to so many roles that he cannot avoid frightening himself with what he himself has dreamed and thought up."

Chelsea is in the process of becoming, and the daily changes in this process keep me constantly surprised. I was asked to describe her personality on the preschool application and couldn't do it. One moment she is independent, the next clinging; an hour of boisterous swinging and climbing alternates with a quiet hour of looking at books or playing with dolls. One night I heard her talking to herself in her room way past bedtime. When I went in she blurted out, "Molly told me she has a new friend and won't play with me anymore." I started plotting solutions: I'd have a talk with Molly; no, I'd call her parents. Then I noticed Chelsea's even breathing; she had given me her troubles and fallen asleep. How could I have been with her all afternoon and not known this was bothering her?

Chelsea can grow two inches and I can't see it until her jeans reach the top of her socks. Sometime between the ages of one and three her hair color turned from blonde to brown and I don't know when it happened. Burton White says of this age, "Babyhood is over. The distance traveled by a three-year-old in terms of human development is staggering." Fitz-hugh Dodson says that the three year old "has passed through the transition from babyhood to true childhood." I have an album full of snapshots, a baby book full of milestones, a shelf full of home movies, and I still feel that I missed seeing the baby turn into a child.

Sometimes Chelsea and I encounter older women who shake their heads when they see us and say, partly to me and partly to themselves, "They grow up so fast." These mothers seem shell-shocked, wondering I suppose what happened to those tiny hands that used to hang on to their fingers. Do all mothers suddenly wake up one day and find their children unrecognizable adults?

The central task of the parent, writes Arnold Gesell, is to "become consistently inquisitive about one permanent question, namely: *'What kind of child is he*—what is his true nature'?" I'm afraid that I will be like all those mothers and find that I didn't know my daughter's true nature at all. But the harder I try to know who Chelsea is, the more she refuses to be known. It is only when I am doing something like cooking that she will sing me a song she learned at preschool or tell me what happened on the playground. In the kitchen I can look at the carrots I'm peeling while she chatters on. If I look at her and ask questions she flees.

To know Chelsea I have to pursue her the way our cat stalks a grasshopper. The cat sits stone still, feigning indiffer-ence for long seconds. But she knows exactly what that grasshopper is up to with every sense she has. When the timing is perfect, the cat pounces, not having twitched a muscle before that to reveal her interest.

One morning, while Chelsea was at preschool, I went into her room to look for clues to who this child really is. In the dollhouse, dishes and furniture lay scrambled in the living room, tiny figures dangled precariously over the edge of the upstairs floor. I couldn't tell if this bedlam was done deliber- ately or the result of neglect. On Chelsea's bed a rag doll had her yarn hair carefully styled with an assortment of Chelsea's barrettes and wore a Christmas tree ornament for a necklace. Under a row of faces drawn on a piece of paper were scrawled attempts at letters, a name for each face. Another paper displayed splotches of the most vibrant colors from the crayon box and a punctured balloon taped in its corner. I am never able to throw away any of these artworks; the shelf in Chelsea's closet is piled with them. I imagine myself sorting through them when she is grown like some puzzled archaeol- ogist, trying to decipher who she was.

Like St. Peter at the Transfiguration who wanted to build shrines to preserve the vision, I want to preserve what I see, bind in time with shrines of mementos what eludes my grasp. But neither Jesus nor a child can be so easily pinned down. Peter saw Jesus with new eyes in a new way and didn't know how to respond. Chelsea is undergoing a contin- ual transfiguration and I spend most of my time as baffled by the appropriate response to the new developments as Peter. As soon as I sort out how to deal with one stage, the next one appears.

Judith Kestenberg writes in *Parenthood,* "Each transi- tion from one phase to the next presents a challenge to both parents and children to give up outdated forms of interaction and to adopt a new system of coexistence. The ability of a parent to meet his side of this challenge depends on his inner preparedness to accept the new image the child forms of him and to erect a new image of his child." I have to be continually discerning what kind of child Chelsea is and yet continually giving up what I discern as she moves on to each new stage of development.

Things seem to work out best when I respond to the person Chelsea is in each moment, whether it's the fairy princess, the independent preschooler, or the tot who hasn't been out of diapers for so very long. According to Bruno Bettelheim in *A Good Enough Parent,* "The beginner in chess, who tries to follow his plans irrespective of his partner's countermoves, will soon go down to defeat. And so will the parent who follows a preconceived plan, based on explanations he received or advice given him for dealing with his child. A parent must continually and flexibly adapt his procedures to the responses of his child, and reassess the everchanging situation as it develops." Once the child has been born, there is no respite. Being a parent requires living in and responding to the dimension of the critical moment, the dimension the child lives in.

I try to see Chelsea as she is at each moment, but so much is in the way: my own childhood, my own parents, what I want to see in her, what I don't want to see. The images I have in my mind of my past and her future distort the living child of the present. In the distortion I miss seeing my child at all and can't respond to the ever-changing situation. A child at this age is infinitely more flexible than an adult according to Burton White who says, "Based on almost three decades of studying human development . . . I do believe the degree of flexibility that humans have, their capacity for fundamental change . . . decline steadily with age."

In addition, the fact that I have grown up, have made choices places me in a different temporal camp from a child who is just beginning to imagine who she is. This difference creates a gulf between us that can never be bridged. When Angela Barron McBride's young daughter wishes that her mother could be her same size so they could play together better, McBride muses, "Wasn't my child putting into words what I always hoped about my parents—that some day we would be friends, equals, and fully understand each other? I yearned to be an adult so we could freely exchange ideas, never realizing that as I grew older they, too, were growing older. We were doomed from the beginning to live in a different piece of time." In *Growing Up* Russell Baker writes about the gap separating him from his son, "Between us there was a dispute about time. He looked upon the time that had been my future in a disturbing way. My future was his past, and being young, he was indifferent to the past."

The dress-up clothes are strewn about the floor in heaps, but Chelsea and I hear the tractor arrive and leave the clothes to go outside and watch. The disker clatters around the hillside, dragging the weeds down in wide swaths. In the spring when the grass was still green, Chelsea and I had a charmed circle in that field where we were completely hidden by tall mustard and blue-eyed grass. The bees collected pollen around us, cloud shapes shifted overhead, and I sat with Chelsea in the warm sun splitting grass blades and watching ladybugs, content with the illusion that things would always remain as they were at that moment. In that circle I imagined that the sun would not set, the flowers wouldn't wither, and that Chelsea would never turn five, or ten, or twenty.

Watching the tractor demolish our circle now, I tell myself that this will help the grass grow again. Chelsea has no regrets. She eagerly welcomes the tractor, just as she welcomes birthdays and the coming of winter rains. I have a predisposition to cling to the status quo. If someone came along and offered me a job as a snake charmer, I would refuse. When I can't entertain the possibilities for change in myself from moment to moment, when I can't see the changes on the hillside from day to day, then I will be fossilized, utterly without the spirit of life. That spirit is contained in Chelsea's dressing up, her chaotic room, her glee in seeing the hill mowed. If I can learn to be a part of that volatile world, maybe I will learn to *see:* when the seasons shift, when something is troubling my child.

I want to stop time, and when I sit in the grass enveloped in autumn or dress up as a fairy princess, time does stop because I am not paying attention to its passing. It is these timeless moments that I live for, but these are the moments a child lives *in*. Wordsworth accounts for a child's kinship with the timeless in his lines, "Not in entire forgetfulness,/ And not in utter nakedness,/But trailing clouds of glory do we come/From God, who is our home. . . ." But we lose this legacy of eternity as we grow, when, according to Annie Dillard, "we start feeling the weight of the atmosphere and learn that there's death in the pot. . . ." We start counting: the days, the hours, the minutes—and lose it all in the counting.

"If we complain of time and take such joy in the seemingly timeless moment," writes Sheldon Vanauken in *A Severe Mercy,* ". . . it suggests that we have not always been or will not always be purely temporal creatures. It suggests that we were created for eternity." What St. Peter saw in the Transfiguration was a glimpse of eternity. That kind of transformation of our limited perception of time is available to humans because we are not purely temporal creatures. It takes seeing as a child sees; maybe that is what Jesus meant when he said that we must become like little children in order to enter the kingdom of heaven.

The dimension of time called the *kairos* is there for us when we can open our eyes enough, and then we are transfigured by it. Madeleine L'Engle calls *kairos* "God's time" and says, "Whenever I have loved most truly and most spontaneously, time has vanished and I have been in *kairos*." When chronological time vanishes, the gulf that separates the generations is transcended. Then the kind of love L'Engle is talking about is possible, the kind that doesn't cling to the person or to the moment.

My child's swift growth makes me more keenly aware of the passage of time than I ever have been; no single moment of a childhood will ever be repeated. The stakes are high; I have only one crack at each of those moments. If I can live with my eyes open, maybe I will not feel as though I have missed the fleeting childhood of my daughter; maybe I will have more evidence than my scrapbooks and photo albums that I knew her.

8. The Breath of Life

The lab technician is trying to fill a vial with blood from my arm, and I can provide only a trickle. "Are you nervous?" she asks me. I can't believe that anyone having a pregnancy test would not be nervous. People are expected to be nervous at their weddings about making a lifetime commitment; why not for the lifetime commitment of having a baby? Having lived through one pregnancy, unanesthetized childbirth, and four years of motherhood, I am decidedly more nervous the second time around, knowing what I am in for.

I go home and wait. The next day a phone call tells me that the test is negative. This is the third negative test I have had in the past year, each one defying what seemed to be the unmistakable symptoms of pregnancy. I am amazed every time that my body can demonstrate with such symptoms my desire for another child and yet not be able to conceive.

Lately, however, I have begun to detect, along with my disappointment accompanying each negative test, an undercurrent of relief as well. I start to suspect my own ambivalence of sabotaging the effort. George's parents have sent us plane tickets to visit them in Hawaii, and I go there determined to sort out my feelings about the matter of having a second child.

The three generations of us stay under the tin roof of an old house on a remote beach of the Big Island. Out of the path of tourists and all but a few fishermen and other local residents willing to navigate the bumpy lava road here, this beach provides a meager supply of playmates for a four year old. When a family does arrive, it is always with more than one child. I observe these siblings who throw sand in each other's eyes and try to drown each other in the surf. Chelsea watches too, envious of their camaraderie. She wants someone to play with besides the parents and grandparents who have limits on how long we are willing to build sand castles or splash with her in the water.

My limits arise partly out of expectations from a pre-child era when I could spend a vacation in a beach chair reading a book. Now, after a game of beach ball catch with Chelsea, I sit down, pick up a book, and she empties a bucket of wet sand on its dry pages. Do I want a second child to play with the first so I can read in peace? My observations of parents with more than one child don't support this fantasy.

I shake the sand out of the book and spread the wet pages to dry. The notion that a second child would automatically follow the first took me completely by surprise. It first appeared when Chelsea was in her twos and Julie from my mother's group became pregnant. Then at family and social gatherings, the subject of a sibling for Chelsea started appearing subtly in conversations. George started musing about how we could rearrange bedroom space in the house to make room for another child. Here I was finally finding some semblance of household order, some time to work, and some time to have real conversations with George and with friends. I couldn't imagine voluntarily plunging back into the maelstrom of sleepless nights and dirty diapers, exacerbated by the needs of the child already here. As Chelsea grows, taking her places has become more fun; we now make regular trips to the zoo and Marine World. The five hour plane ride here was a special occasion with a four year old, not the ordeal it would have been with an infant or toddler.

As Joyce Maynard writes in *Domestic Affairs,* "The odd thing is: The moment when suddenly you want a baby is likely to come precisely when your life seems so good the way it is. And having a baby is the one thing that's guaranteed to change it." Maybe it was because life seemed "do-able" once more that I started to think about a second child. Or maybe I got caught up in the excitement of the pregnancy of Julie and then of other friends expecting a second child and wanted to relive the thrill of giving birth to an entirely new and unique human being. When mothers I knew delivered their babies, I could hold the newborns with experienced arms, feeling some competence now that begged to be used.

It is hard for me to determine how much of my desire for another child is my own and how much is wanting to join the excitement, to please George, to please the grandparents. Do I want to be the fussed over and revered mother of a newborn again? Do I want the relatively known challenges of a baby to make me feel competent in the face of the unfamiliar challenges of a four year old?

I think of the times when I felt as though I couldn't listen to Chelsea's chatter for another minute and the times she made me so angry I had to lock myself in my bedroom to keep from hitting her. Would having two children push my patience over the brink, make me into a mother who is always yelling at her kids—or who hits them? Would having another child be better for Chelsea—or would it make her life worse? Although I am grateful for my two younger sisters now that I am an adult, maybe I remember too well the feelings of a first child who has her place usurped by a new arrival.

I have heard all my life from my mother about her loneliness as an only child, but maybe it didn't have to be that way. Preschool and invitations to play provide plenty of playmates for Chelsea; maybe we only need to take vacations where there are more children. Sharryl Hawke and David Knox found that the prospective parents they interviewed for their book, *One Child by Choice,* over a four year period believed "that having one child is not fair to the child . . . that something is missed when a family unit has only one child . . . that there is something inherently 'wrong' with having a single child." Hawke and Knox produce studies and arguments showing the advantages of having a single child, but it is hard not to be taken in by the "widespread belief that a single child is disadvantaged." This belief, these authors assert, is what "motivates many couples to have a second child."

George had no siblings, and, like my mother, does not want a child of his to repeat the experience. I can't help feeling that I have let him down with all these negative pregnancy tests. Neither his parents nor mine ask any direct questions on the subject, but what is unspoken hangs in the air.

When Jane Lazarre considers the possibility of a second child she laughs at herself and what she calls in *The Mother Knot* "my recurring attraction for illusions despite even my own undeniable experience. . . ." It seems, however, that some illusions are required in order to have babies, just as illusions help make the commitment to marriage. It is easier to commit myself to another baby with the image of an infant cooing to my lullaby, just as making the marriage commitment is easier with the image of an eternal honeymoon. The problems arise in trying to preserve the illusions: not letting the infant grow up—or not accepting the post-honeymoon stage of marriage.

Alice Walker tells of her mother advising her, when Alice's daughter was a year old, to have another one soon to give the first someone to play with and "so you can get it all over with faster." Walker replies, "Such advice does not come from what a woman recalls of her own experience. It comes from a pool of such misguidance women have collected over the millennia to help themselves feel less foolish for having more than one child. This pool is called, desperately, pitiably, 'Women's Wisdom'. In fact, it should be called 'Women's Folly'." The truth is, I am having trouble separating the wisdom from the folly, what I want from what everyone else seems to want, and which Chelsea needs more: a sibling or a sane mother.

Lazarre hears two voices warring within her. One voice says ". . . the more children you have, the more deadly becomes the destruction of your independent soul." It is this possibility that makes me fear losing my individuality, becoming completely taken over by my children. But Lazarre's other voice answers, "The daily grinding friction of motherhood will give you the chance, at least, of relinquishing some of your egotism. You will finally cease to be a child." Having more children demands a selflessness I don't know if I can muster. It could be that I am clinging to what independence and freedom I have carved out and fearing the rigors of further changes a new angel would ask.

The authors of *Our Selves and Our Children* conclude, "The issue of how many children to have is obscured by myths and social attitudes. . . . We have heard about the lonely only child and the spoiled only child and the high-strung only child. We've also heard about the mixed-up middle child and the forgotten fourth child. However . . . the decision to have or not to have more than one child has less to do with facts and figures or expert opinions than with deep inner feelings about how we want our lives to be, what we expect for ourselves, and what practical things we can do to arrange our lives in a way that suits us and our existing family." How *do* I want my life to be? Filled with the adventure as well as the chaos of children? Or do I need more spaces in the chaos, more reflection than adventure?

Chelsea just brought a bucket of sea water to me, and instead of dumping it on my book this time, she left its collection of tide pool life in my care while she went off for a swim with George. The three different kinds of crabs in the bucket are now fighting while the two tiny fish try to stay out of their way. One crab pries a pincer off another. Nasty business, this living together in a bucket when the whole ocean is your home. I lower a rock to the bottom and it seems to divert them. Would one more child in our family set us nipping at each other like these crabs?

Now George and Chelsea emerge from the water. As George stretches out on his towel, Chelsea begins to dig in the sand, creating her own world with moats and dams. I can't hear what she is saying, but her lips move in a continual commentary, just as when she plays alone with her dolls.

Maybe she is learning that it is not such a bad thing to be by yourself. That something happens in solitude that cannot happen in the midst of company and commotion. On this remote beach, the importance of solitude seems apparent to me. But so much is apparent here on this island. I can stand in shallow water and look through a mask to see a galaxy of fish; I don't even have to swim to find them. I watch distant clouds blow away, and the tip of a volcano appears. Mangoes dangle from roadside branches; coconuts crash to the ground in the night.

On the edge of this volcano, we are witnesses to cre-ation. It is apparent how the dry land appeared, pushing itself up through the waters that covered the earth; how the fiery lava slammed into the sea, then crumbled and brought forth vegetation to feed the people and animals who appeared when the rock had cooled. Looking down the unpeopled shoreline, I see this island as it was centuries and aeons ago, something I don't see on the crowded beaches near the big hotels. In *The Measure of My Days* Florida Scott-Maxwell observes, "It is undeniable that one needs the absence of others to enjoy the magic of many things." One of those things is inner clarity, the chance to find out what Rilke calls "the uninterrupted news that grows out of silence." Maybe in the solitude of this place I can find out what that news is for me.

At sunset two young boys who have been splashing in the water suddenly stand as if at attention to watch the sun drop off the edge of the earth. As soon as the last golden sliver disappears, they resume their play as if they had never stopped.

This ritual pause to stand in awe that seems so natural here would be out of place at home. I can't imagine commute traffic pulling off the side of the freeway to watch the sun set. According to Madeleine L'Engle in *Walking on Water,* the ancient Hawaiians called the Caucasian missionaries who arrived to convert them "haoles," meaning "without breath" because they said their prayers without the long pauses that the Hawaiians knew were necessary to breathe life into them.

71

It seems that this quiet, listening aspect of prayer is more important than anything I might say. So I, a haole, try to be still and listen.

"There is only one birth," says Meister Eckhart, "— and this birth takes place in the being and in the ground and core of the soul. . . . The fruitful person gives birth out of the very same foundation from which the Creator begets the eternal Word. It is from this core that one becomes fruitfully pregnant." The real question is then, as co-creator, am I fruitful, do I bear fruit from the ground and core of my soul?

One day Chelsea blurted out in the way that children do, "I think we should love each other as much as we can." Bearing fruit is not so much about how many children I have as much as about whether I love the one I have as much as I can. It is whether what I do comes from the same spirit as the Creator's. To do that I need what Fox calls "silent spaces and silent times—the spaces between the drumbeats and the heartbeats. . . ." Here on this beach, those spaces come easily in watching the surf crash on the rocks, the fishermen pull in their nets. "Were we worshiping outdoors more often," Fox writes, "the silence would come naturally as it does whenever native people gather to worship."

I think the person I was created to be requires more silent spaces than adventure. This is difficult to admit in a culture that values action over meditation. "Silence receives too little appreciation," says Scott-Maxwell, "silence being a higher, rarer thing than sound. Silence implies inner riches, and a savoring of impressions. Babies value this too. They lie silent, and one can suppose them asleep, but look closer, and with eyes wide open they are sparkling like jewels in the dark." Here on this beach, without the noise of television or traffic, we all have a chance to sparkle like that once again.

It is almost dark now, and a pair of fins, probably those of a manta ray, slowly slices the calm water. I read that more volcanoes will emerge one day from the waters to the south. Creation continues and I might as well learn to watch and listen in order that I might discover my role in it.

Chelsea and George have decided to return the crea-tures of the bucket into the rising tide. After a wave recedes, we each carefully place a crab on the rocks. Just before the next wave crashes over them, they scurry for cover. Never hesitating, they appear to know exactly where to hide.

I would like to be that certain of where I belong in creation. But there is no such thing as certainty; being a mother has taught me that at least. All I can do is to be still and listen to the voice within. Good cases can be made for or against any number of children, and the fact remains that I have not been able to conceive a second time. Reason does not have the final say here. The question of whether and how I am to bear fruit has to be answered from that deep center of my being where the heart, soul, mind, and body are one with the Creator.

9. The Sins of the Mothers

Chelsea waves at me from the top of the highest spiral slide in the park, the same slide I waved at my mother from when I was four years old. I close my eyes and it all comes back: the tingle of fear at pushing off over the steep edge, the thrill of the whirling descent between the high metal sides, and the relief at seeing the park reappear when my feet touched the sand. I open my eyes and my child is standing in front of me, wanting to go back up again.

We are visiting this park in the town I grew up in to reconnoiter for Chelsea's five year old birthday party. The party guests will ride the train the twenty miles here from home, have a birthday picnic at this park, and return by rail. This plan grew out of Chelsea's current infatuation with trains and my nostalgia for the park I played in as a child.

When Chelsea has tested all the playground equipment and we have surveyed the picnic area, I have a sudden impulse to drive the mile or so to the house I lived in until I was ten. Passing through the once familiar streets and pointing out the neighborhood landmarks to my daughter, I turn onto the little cul-de-sac and stop in front of the second house from the corner. I marvel that this tiny house is here at all; like the park, this entire street seems more like a place I have traveled back to in time than a reality in the present.

Chelsea, who has a hard time believing that I was ever a

74

child, is agog at seeing the house my mother brought me home to from the hospital, the street I learned to roller skate and ride a bicycle on. I show her the places I built forts with the neighbor kids, the garage I gave magic shows in, and I can hardly believe it myself. That little girl seems to have changed beyond recognition, yet the person I am now was formed by the experiences that little girl had in this house and on this block.

My mother too must have been formed and changed by her life here. She was young and expecting me when she and my father bought this house with green shutters and a white picket fence. She sewed curtains for the windows and filled the flower beds with gladiolas and delphiniums. In such a cottage I can see my mother's dreams for living happily ever after. The green shutters of the house are now taupe and the picket fence is gone, but my mother's dreams live on in me and in my daughter sitting here beside me.

One block away from here is the house my maternal grandmother and great-grandmother lived in, forming a community of four generations of mothers and daughters. The wedded bliss these grandmothers had been raised to expect from life had been thwarted by failed marriages, and they looked to my mother to achieve their dream. To accomplish this, my mother dedicated herself completely to caring for her husband and three children.

To all appearances it seemed that here, in this house, my parents did live happily ever after. It certainly was an idyllic place for a child to grow up, with a school my sisters and I could walk to at one end of the block, the sidewalks and backyards always filled with playmates, and my mother always available to deliver a forgotten lunch or to nurse a scraped knee.

It is only looking back on it now that I see how costly living that dream was for my mother. In assuming responsibility for creating a happy family and a smooth-running household, she put aside her own interests and her own feelings—it was part of the deal. Bit by bit she gave up tiny shards of herself for her family until she hardly knew where she ended and we began. My father went on hunting and fishing trips, my sisters and I went to dancing lessons and Brownie day camp, and my mother saw that we all had clean clothes to put on and a hot dinner when we got home. She would say that her family was her interest, that our highs and lows were her feelings. She was doing what she had been raised to do and she would say that she was happy.

But the youthful exuberance that I see in pictures of my parents as newlyweds and with which I imagine my mother filled the flower beds and sewed the curtains for this house disappeared, swallowed up by what came to be for her the labor of duty rather than passion. Her children played and learned and her husband built up a family business with fervent intensity, but that intensity slowly drained out of my mother. Eventually, she seemed to be just going through the motions, worn out by the impossible task of fulfilling all of our needs.

I must have sensed that something was missing in my mother's life because hers was a role I worked vehemently to avoid. As a child I became a tomboy who refused to play with dolls, avoided the kitchen, and vowed never to wear lipstick or have babies. I perceived that my father had more status and clout in the world as well as in the family and I sought his approval of my pursuits rather than my mother's. I have spent much of my adult life trying not to be like my mother, to make my life different from hers. We live isolated in the hills now because I didn't want to live in this kind of suburban tract that she chose. I was married for eight years before the idea of having a baby ever even occurred to me.

I could finally entertain the notion of becoming a mother myself because I felt sufficiently separated from my own mother to believe I could do it differently. Unlike her, I had finished college and graduate school and made my way in the working world for ten years. I felt ready for spending weekdays in the vegetable garden, pushing a stroller in the park. As soon as I became a mother, however, I saw that my efforts to separate myself from my own mother had been all on the surface. Despite my efforts to live a different kind of life, even to be a different kind of mother, I sensed that I was becoming like her. It was as if I had inherited the unshakable conviction that her way was the right way, the only way, to be a mother.

"It is from mothers that daughters first learn what is expected of them as females in society, what 'femininity' is," Signe Hammer writes in *Daughters and Mothers/Mothers and Daughters*. "In our culture femininity implies dependency, nonassertiveness, and a tendency to live in and through others—to rely more on relationships than on one's sense of oneself." This is the legacy my mother inherited from her mother and grandmother, a legacy that demanded a submissiveness to the needs of her husband and children on whom she depended for her identity and *raison d'être*. The problem with dependency is explored by Collette Dowling in *The Cinderella Complex*. "Dependency," she says, "by its very nature, creates self-doubt, and self-doubt can lead all too quickly to self-hatred." This legacy of the mother, writes Adrienne Rich, "mutilates the daughter who watches her for clues as to what it means to be a woman. Like the traditional foot-bound Chinese woman, she passes on her own affliction. The mother's self-hatred and low expectations are the binding-rags for the psyche of the daughter."

I should not have been so surprised that I would feel the binding rags when I became a mother myself. Taking care of children is not as valued in our culture as remunerative work. It is society's devaluation of that role that gave my mother the sense of inferiority which led to her self-effacement. Caring for children is also an all-consuming task. A child takes over one's thoughts, one's inner equilibrium, one's very identity. It is much easier for the primary caretaker to give in and be taken over than to fight back for the right to an individual self. These snares are inherent in motherhood, but trying to do the job in a way that is different from the way my mother did it raises additional conflicts. Dowling writes, "The terrible confusion women are experiencing about femininity is strongly related to our choosing not to live like our mothers. Psychiatrists have begun to discover that the more confined and dependent our mothers, the more anxious we'll be about pushing off in directions that are different."

The confusion is exacerbated by a sense of guilt about my mother's self-sacrifice. Inherent in my mother's service of her daughters was the expectation that we would make her proud, would give her back the self she gave up. This resulted in a tangled web of her desires for me and what I wanted for myself. I will never get the strands completely sorted out in my lifetime, but making the attempt helps me see how Chelsea is being woven into the web.

It was a bad sign that I wanted only a daughter. When I was pregnant, I refused to consider the possibility of having a boy, not even picking out a boy's name. Signe Hammer tells of a woman who says of wanting only a daughter, "I wanted an extension of myself, another me, a happier me, a more successful me. . . . The danger in this kind of fantasizing is, of course, that a mother will overidentify with her daughter, living so intensely through her that she places an impossible burden of expectation on her." This overidentification is the sin of the totally self-sacrificing mother, the inevitable result of giving up one's being for that of another.

I see my own overidentification when my pride in Chelsea's accomplishments becomes competitiveness, and I find myself wanting my daughter to be the smartest, the most talented, the most popular, even in preschool. I see it when I am thrilled by her successes and crushed by her failures. When *she* misbehaves, I wonder what *I* did wrong. My own success or failure in life seems mixed up with what Chelsea does or doesn't do. This is too much of a burden on a child and deprives her from taking responsibility for her own success and happiness in life. It is also too much of a burden on a mother to devote her life to making her child happy and successful. My child needs unconditional love to develop healthy self-esteem, not love that is conditional on how well she performs in accordance with my expectations.

In *Perfect Women,* Dowling says that her first-born child, a girl, "was to reflect glory back on me. If she were wonderful it would mean, somehow, that I was wonderful. If she were truly awesome, it would break the chain of insecurity, and doubt, and self-contempt that had been passed on in our family from one generation of women to the next. My mother's feelings of insecurity and her struggle to deny them, my own struggles, my grandmother's—all would be given meaning by . . . nothing less than the female Messiah!" This reliance on the new generation to redeem the sins of the mothers only perpetuates the transgressions. The web can

only be disentangled before it is allowed to become too en-
meshing in the first place. Otherwise, as Nancy Friday
writes in *My Mother/My Self,* "Daughters who have tried to
live out their mother's dreams end up with a diminished self.
Little is ever felt . . . because the daughter has always been
her mother's extension and not her own person. . . . The
primary rule is always that a mother can't go wrong, *ever,* by
encouraging her child after age one and a half to be as individuated and separated as possible." A mother can't do this,
however, unless she herself has an individuated and separated
self of her own. Real self-sacrifice is only possible if one has
developed a strong self to sacrifice. Living through others
cannot be of real service to them.

Now that I am a mother, however, I understand how
this loss of self can happen. After giving birth to a new life,
all other pursuits seem insignificant. The infant's needs have
to come first or she won't survive. It is a mother's greatest
temptation, especially as more children come along, to continue to put the children always before herself. In *The Way
of All Women* Esther Harding remarks, "It is of little use to
(the children) to have the most perfect physical care unless
their mother is a vital woman deeply fulfilled in her own
life." Living through one's children is the sin of overmothering that comes from a mother who neglects her own needs.
But Harding also states, "Maternity is a serious and arduous
undertaking, and those who are not prepared to make personal sacrifices for it are in no position to attempt it." Not
making the necessary sacrifices is the sin of neglect that
comes from a mother too preoccupied with her own pursuits
or too overwhelmed by her own troubles to give her children
the attention they need. Being the primary caretaker of a
child creates fertile ground for one sin or another to flourish.

The sin of overmothering is the result of trying to live an impossible dream that is built on an unrealistic idealization of the mother and her job. Angela Barron McBride describes it in this way: "Women, and most especially mothers, are not chained to present roles by visions of female subservience, but by the notion that they have the inherent where-with-all to keep everybody 'happy', to charm away aggressive feelings with a lullaby, to soothe tired souls, pointing out the joy of day-to-day living. The ties that bind are not so much shackles of male chauvinism as ribbons of fairy-tale thinking." The mothers who raised their children on this block believed in the fairy tale and worked hard to make it come true in their families. The mothers' role included sharing the blame for their children's failures and the credit for their successes. But these mothers needed some definition of themselves beyond their children, for their own sake and for the sake of their children. Particularly the daughters needed more than one dominant influence in our lives. Otherwise we had to act out of rebellion rather than from a solid inner sense of self to keep from turning into our mothers when we grew up.

The problem for the daughters was that the mothers who gave their lives to their children accepted the subordination of the role that the culture gave those who took care of others. My mother *did* have less status and clout than my father who went out in the world to make a living. As a result, she had little self-confidence and a lot of insecurity about who she was and what she could do. It is only now that I see the enormity of the job my mother did: raising three children as well as caring for the grandmothers as they aged, her father when he got cancer and moved in with us, and, later, a demanding mother-in-law. I wish she hadn't felt compelled to hide her own feelings so she could be the one everyone else could count on, wish that she could have shown the frustration, anger, sadness, and resentment she must have felt sometimes. I wish she had valued herself enough to know the importance of what she was doing, to acknowledge at least the arduousness of her job.

Because my mother accepted her culture's judgment of the inferiority of her "feminine" tasks, I rejected those qualities associated with the feminine side of the personality, what Riane Eisler in *The Chalice and the Blade* calls the "life-sustaining labor of nurturing, helping and loving others." These are the feminine virtues that Eisler says have been devalued and rejected by our culture in favor of the "masculine virtues of toughness, aggressiveness, and dominance." But it is the "feminine virtues," Eisler says, that Jesus taught must be elevated "from a secondary or supportive to a primary and central position. We must not be violent but instead turn the other cheek; we must do unto others as we would have them do unto us; we must love our neighbors and even our enemies. Instead of . . . toughness, aggressiveness, and dominance, what we must value above all else are mutual responsibility, compassion, gentleness, and love."

This message of "spiritual equality" Eisler sees as essential not only to a positive self-image for women but for the very survival of a human race now threatened by "masculine technologies of destruction" and a "dominator approach to conflict." In Eisler's dream "caring for others is not just given lip service but is the most highly rewarded, and therefore most highly valued, human activity."

It is this dream of a strong feminine that I have for my daughter and her generation. I dream of a culture in which men and women can incorporate both feminine and masculine virtues into their lives, in which both men and women can care for others and find respect in the world. It would be a culture that gives real value and respect to those who most need caring for, children and the elderly, as well as to those who care for them.

Betty Friedan describes in *The Second Stage* her dream for women of the next generation: They will have "the right to have a child, joyously, responsibly, without paying a terrible price of isolation from the world and its rewarded occupations, its decisions and actions. . . . The daughters will go farther than we could envision. They will be new kinds of women, different from their mothers, as I was different from mine. . . . They already have strengths we lacked, and feelings they are not afraid of . . . as well as opportunities and supports from society itself now, role models and affirmation from other women, and different expectations from the men in their lives."

For Dowling, the dream reclaims passion lost by living through others. "Ultimately," she says in *The Cinderella Complex,* "the goal is emotional spontaneity—an inner liveliness that pervades everything we do, every work project, every social encounter, every love relationship. It comes from the conviction that I am the first force in my life." This is what was missing from my mother's life and what was such a struggle for me to hold on to when I became a mother.

I think my mother wanted something different for my sisters and me, a different kind of life, but she couldn't give us a clue about how to attain it. Each generation wants something better for the next, something not even yet envisioned. My dream is for Chelsea to grow up not rejecting the feminine side of herself as I did for so long, for her to see all the possibilities of life open to her and actively choose her own path among them, for her to dream her own dream and make it come true. My role in this is to reject the temptation to define myself totally as mother and live through Chelsea, to help my daughter find other people whom she can learn from and model herself on, to learn to value the feminine in myself and in others. If I can do these things, Chelsea will have a chance to live her own life, free from the sins of her mother.

10. Exodus

We sold the house in the hills. The once-abandoned rock quarry nearby began operating again, and we were driven out by the noise, dust, and truck traffic. When the house was empty, I brought Chelsea back for a last look at her room, the vegetable garden, the hillside. From the deck I watched the retreating sun burnish the eastern hills bronze and made sure I had memorized the trees we planted: apricots, almonds, cherries, apple, and peach.

Chelsea pulled at me to leave. She came newborn to this house, took her first step here, said her first word here. But her tire swing was gone, her room empty; nothing here was "do-able" for her any longer. She was as puzzled by my tears as I was by her eagerness to leave.

We are temporarily renting a house on a busy street near town. The traffic noise is worse than the quarry trucks, and from the windows we view fences and neighbors' walls instead of hillsides and fruit trees. Chelsea loves it here. From the front porch she watches fire engines, ambulances, buses, traffic jams, runners, and cyclists. To her it is like living on the edge of a parade.

As soon as we arrived, Chelsea learned to ride her two-wheel bicycle on the sidewalk in front of our house. She says she always wanted a sidewalk. Not only are sidewalks good for bike riding but for roller skating, hopscotch, and lemonade stands. Even better than all this to her, though, is a friend next door. Chelsea and her friend can call to each other over the fence and play at a moment's notice as I could with my childhood neighbors.

I miss our trail and the tall grass on the hill, but I feel less isolated here, more a part of the human race, both the best and the worst of it. We see friends more here, because our location between an expressway and a freeway puts us on the road to almost everywhere in and out of town. But I also have answered the door to people who appear to be casing our house for burglary and to girls from the nearby junior college cross country team who wanted me to call the police because they recognized the car of a man who exposes himself to them along their route. We keep our bicycles locked in the garage here, the doors to the house bolted. I pore over newspaper accounts of child abductions, and don't let Chelsea and her friends play on the sidewalk unsupervised.

Tomorrow Chelsea starts kindergarten and she is as excited about plunging into school as she was about moving into town. At school, as on this street, there is much I want to protect her from. But my job is to teach her to protect herself, from physical harm as well as from the hurtful remarks of other children. She has to learn to be realistic without being afraid, to be tough without being a bully.

I worry that school rules and curriculum will replace my child's sense of wonder and free-spirited play, that pressure for grades will squelch her natural curiosity. According to Erik Erikson, however, school provides the structure necessary for a child at this stage to develop a "sense of industry." At school, says Erikson, "play is transformed into work, game into competition and cooperation, and the freedom of imagination into the duty to perform with full attention to the techniques which make imagination communicable, account-able, and applicable to defined tasks." In going to school, Chelsea will learn to make connections with the larger world and find her place in it. I just hope she can retain something of that "beginner's mind" she was born with so that her work will always be infused with a spirit of playfulness.

Tonight George is conducting Chelsea's hair washing, and I am out in the backyard to escape the heat of the Indian summer and shed my tears at this bench mark in the separa-tion process. I can hear Chelsea's whoops and yells from the open bathroom window, a revelation of how much our new neighbors hear of our voices which were used to shouting freely to the hills. A child who adds new words to her vocab-ulary and new motor skills to her repertoire every day wel-comes change much better than I do. It is the right time for Chelsea to start school, just as it was the right time for us to move, but I can't help crying a little over losing the baby I used to carry around with me, just as I cried over leaving the house the baby first came home to. Good-byes have to be made, the close of a stage marked, before I can move on.

Last spring I waited outside of the classroom while the teacher tested Chelsea for her readiness to begin kindergar-ten. I sat nervously, feeling that my competence as a parent would be judged on whether my child would be able to match shapes, recognize colors, and skip. But a better test of parental competence would measure how well I am meeting the challenges this particular child presents. How well am I identifying and working through the problems that come up day after day in raising a child? To the extent that I am confronting rather than avoiding the problems of daily life, I am teaching Chelsea to do so and giving her something as valuable as the development of cognitive and motor skills.

Mastering these skills is important, as Erikson points out, but how well a child performs is often emphasized over how well she is learning to meet the frustrations that will arise in the larger world where she is not protected by her parents. Instead of worrying about how she will perform in school, I should welcome the opportunity that school will provide Chelsea to work through both the intentional challenges of the curriculum and the unintentional challenges of the playground. "It is in this whole process of meeting and solving problems that life has its meaning," says M. Scott Peck. "Problems call forth our courage and wisdom; indeed, they create our courage and wisdom. It is only because of problems that we grow mentally and spiritually. When we desire to encourage the growth of the human spirit, we challenge and encourage the human capacity to solve problems, just as in school we deliberately set problems for our children to solve. It is through the pain of confronting and resolving problems that we learn."

It must be a universal tendency for parents to want to protect children from life's difficulties, but it does their offspring no favor. D.W. Winnicott points out that it is "the good-enough mother's carefully calibrated *failure* of adaptation, her failure to give him everything he needs, that permits her child slowly . . . slowly to learn to tolerate frustration, to acquire a sense of reality and to learn to get some of what he needs for himself." In the same way it is the inability of a teacher with a classroom full of children to meet every child's needs all of the time that teaches the children to rely on themselves more, to learn to make their own attempt on the problems that confront them. Parents can do a better job of taking a child step by step through the process of problem solving, but school gives children a chance to rise to challenges without parental hand holding. Emphasizing a child's performance doesn't allow for the mistakes that are an important and inevitable part of the process.

Fairy tales also teach a child about this process, according to Bruno Bettelheim in *The Uses of Enchantment*. He says that fairy tales convey to a child that "a struggle against severe difficulties in life is unavoidable, is an intrinsic part of human existence—but that if one does not shy away, but steadfastly meets unexpected and often unjust hardships, one masters all obstacles and at the end emerges victorious." Fairy tales do not try to shelter children from the dark side of human nature that lurks outside of my front door as well as in me and in my child. Bettelheim says, "There is a widespread refusal to let children know that the source of much that goes wrong in life is due to our very own natures—the propensity of all men for acting aggressively, asocially, selfishly, out of anger and anxiety. Instead, we want our children to believe that, inherently, all men are good. But children know that *they* are not always good; and often, even when they are, they would prefer not to be. This contradicts what they are told by their parents, and therefore makes the child a monster in his own eyes."

Living in a family brings out that side of our nature that can be more easily hidden from acquaintances and strangers. It is better for a child to see her parents' struggle with that nature than to believe that she is the only one to act in anger or out of selfishness. Before we sold our house, we had to sand a grape juice stain off of the wooden window seat in the dining room. The stain was put there when I threw the contents of my glass in anger at George one night during dinner while Chelsea gaped. I was fortunate to be drinking something so indelible as grape juice because for almost three years that purple mark was a daily reminder for me to control my anger. How else can I expect Chelsea not to throw things at people when *she* is angry? Ultimately, Chelsea is going to deal with frustration in the way she sees her parents deal with it, day after day, year after year.

A child makes me see what I need to change about myself. As I work on making these changes, I teach Chelsea something about the process of confronting problems. If she sees me laboring at this process, then she learns that this is what humans do, this is a normal part of existence. In meeting my own needs, I serve hers, and the conflict between them blurs. As Peck puts it, "It is actually impossible to forsake our own spiritual development in favor of someone else's. We cannot forsake self-discipline and at the same time be disciplined in our care for another. We cannot be a source of strength unless we nurture our own strength. . . . Not only do self-love and love of others go hand in hand but . . . ultimately they are indistinguishable."

Having to change the way I function is tedious and painful work. It is easier to try to "fix" Chelsea than to work on myself. But a child won't be "fixed" or molded, and the harder I try, the more I am faced with my own need to be in control, my own lack of faith. A child does not fit neatly into preconceived plans; she sounds the alarm and destroys preconceptions. What Florida Scott-Maxwell says about life applies to a child: "Life does not accommodate you, it shatters you. It is meant to, and it couldn't do it better. Every seed destroys its container or else there would be no fruition." Becoming a parent means more than accepting the daily destruction of neatly laid plans and schedules. It means welcoming the destruction of what is comfortable but harmful in my relationships and the destruction of the effort to maintain a veneer of invulnerability in the face of life's obstacles.

In *How To Be a Mother and a Person Too* Shirley Radl says that most of the mothers she talked to "agreed that it took about five years of continual chaos, confusion, and feelings of inadequacy for them to reach their breaking points. That reconciles rather nicely," she says, "with sociologist Jessie Bernard's contention that it takes only about five years of motherhood to completely break someone." The breaking point is the place where grace can come through. When I feel that I have things under control, then I can have no faith. When I know I can't control my anger or can't control what happens to my child at school, then I can pray. A child who is changing so rapidly can bring parents to their breaking points in a new way every day. To have faith is to experience God's presence in this struggle with the angel.

What I want to pass on to Chelsea above all is the knowledge that life's struggles are worth engaging in because of that presence. I cannot give her my faith; she will have to find her own, but I can try to convey to her something of the experience of grace. In *With a Daughter's Eye* Mary Catherine Bateson says that her mother, Margaret Mead, "did not present me with a set of doctrines in which to believe, but set out to make sure that I knew what it would feel like to believe, for the great gap between those for whom faith is a living force and those for whom it is an irrelevance is not a disagreement about fact but an incommensurate way of experiencing." Living with my whole heart, through both joy and adversity, is to experience faith. It requires a willingness to be shattered, to live with full awareness of what it means to be human.

It is that experience of life in its heights and depths that will determine Chelsea's capacity for faith more than any facts about religion I can teach her. In *Will Our Children Have Faith?* John Westerhoff writes, "We are not saved by our knowledge, our beliefs, or our worship in the church; just as we are not saved by our actions or our religion. We are saved by the anguish and love of God and to live according to that is to have faith." The experience of a God who suffers with me, of a God who loves me unconditionally enables me to pass through the refining fire of parenting and be trans-formed by it. Passing on that unconditional love to my child is my central task, the one that will shape the way Chelsea sees her place in the world. According to Peck, "If we have loving, forgiving parents, we are likely to believe in a loving, forgiving God. And in our adult view the world is likely to seem as nurturing a place as our childhood was. If our parents were harsh and punitive, we are likely to mature with a con-cept of a harsh and punitive monster-god. And if they failed to care for us, we will likely envision the universe as similarly uncaring."

I squint up into the night sky to get my bearings, but the stars are obscured by the brightness of street lights. I rarely catch a glimpse of the moon these days, and have lost track of what phase it is in. An exodus always results in some time spent in the wilderness. Now that I have wandered over the terrain of motherhood this far, I see things already I would have done differently. I would have laughed more, let Chel-sea eat more marshmallows, spent more time lolling on the hillside. I would have yelled less, worried less, and expected less of myself during the roughest times. Parents have to figure out our own path as we go and make course adjust-ments along the way.

Now Chelsea begins her journey into the wilderness of the larger world and has to learn to get her bearings. She will find mountains to scale and long stretches of desert. I would like to be able to hand her an itinerary to the Promised Land, but the only tools I can give her to navigate with are the ones I live by myself. During her school years, I can travel with her, point out some of the landmarks and pitfalls, and help her up when she falls. As she ventures into life, she'll carry the blind spots and blunders of her parents as baggage. And then, in not too many years, if we haven't weighted her down too much, she'll be charting her own course, forging her own path.

As Moses could not complete the journey to the Promised Land with his people, neither can parents travel with our children to their destinations in life. Tomorrow is a step for Chelsea toward making the journey her own. I will send her off with loud hosannas, rejoicing that this angel is passing my way.

References

Baker, Russell. *Growing Up.* New York: Congdon and Weed, Inc., 1982.

Bateson, Mary Catherine. *With a Daughter's Eye.* New York: William Morrow and Co., Inc., 1984.

Becker, Ernest. *The Denial of Death.* New York: Macmillan Publishing Co., Inc., 1973.

Benedek, Therese. "The Family as a Psychologic Field." In *Parenthood: Its Psychology and Psychopathology,* edited by E. James Anthony and Therese Benedek. Boston: Little, Brown and Company, 1970.

Berends, Polly Berrien. *Whole Child/Whole Parent.* New York: Harper and Row, Publishers, Inc., 1975.

Bettelheim, Bruno. *A Good Enough Parent.* New York: Alfred A. Knopf, 1987.

———— *The Uses of Enchantment.* New York: Random House, 1977.

Boston Women's Health Book Collective, The. *Our Selves and Our Children.* New York: Random House, 1978.

Brazelton, T. Berry. *Infants and Mothers.* New York: Dell Publishing Co., Inc., 1969.

Buber, Martin. *I and Thou.* New York: Charles Scribner's Sons, 1970.

Burck, Frances Wells. *Mothers Talking.* New York: St. Martin's Press, 1986.

De Castillejo, Irene Claremont. *Knowing Woman.* New York: Harper and Row, 1974.

Dillard, Annie. *Pilgrim at Tinker Creek.* New York: Bantam Books, Inc., 1974.

Dodson, Fitzhugh. *How to Parent.* New York: New American Library, 1970.

Dowling, Collette. *The Cinderella Complex.* New York: Simon and Schuster, Inc., 1981.

———— *Perfect Women.* New York: Simon and Schuster, Inc., 1988.

Eisler, Riane. *The Chalice and the Blade.* San Francisco: Harper and Row, 1987.

Elkind, David. *The Hurried Child.* Reading, Massachusetts: Addison-Wesley Publishing Co., 1981.

Erikson, Erik H. *Childhood and Society.* New York: W.W. Norton and Co., Inc., 1963.

Farson, Richard. Quoted by Flora Davis in "Are You Trying to Be Too Good a Parent?" *Redbook,* April 1977.

Fox, Matthew. *The Coming of the Cosmic Christ.* San Francisco: Harper and Row, 1988.

———— *Meditations with Meister Eckhart.* Santa Fe, New Mexico: Bear and Co., 1982.

Friday, Nancy. *My Mother/My Self.* New York: Delacorte Press, 1977.

Friedan, Betty. *The Second Stage.* New York: Summit Books, 1981.

Gesell, Arnold, Frances L. Ilg, and Louise Bate Ames, *Infant and Child in the Culture of Today.* rev. ed. New York: Harper and Row, 1974.

Greenspan, Stanley I., and Nancy Thorndike Greenspan. *First Feelings.* New York: Viking Penguin, Inc. 1985.

Hammer, Signe. *Daughters and Mothers/Mothers and Daughters.* New York: Quadrangle/The New York Times Book Co., 1975.

Harding, Esther. *The Way of All Women.* rev. ed. New York: G.P. Putnam Sons, 1970.

Hawke, Sharryl, and David Knox. *One Child by Choice.* Englewood Cliffs, New Jersey: Prentice-Hall, Inc., 1977.

Hochschild, Arlie Russell. *The Second Shift.* New York: Viking, 1989.

Isaacs, Susan, and Marti Keller. *The Inner Parent.* New York: Harcourt Brace Jovanovich, 1979.

Jung, C.G. *Answer to Job.* Translated by R.F.C. Hull. Cleveland, Ohio: The World Publishing Company, 1960.

Kestenberg, Judith. "The Effect on Parents of the Child's Transition into and out of Latency." In *Parenthood: Its Psychology and Psychopathology,* edited by E. James Anthony and Therese Benedek. Boston: Little, Brown, and Company, 1970.

Kübler-Ross, Elisabeth. *On Children and Death.* New York: Macmillan Publishing Co., 1983.

Kushner, Harold S. *When Bad Things Happen to Good People.* New York: Schocken Books, 1981.

L'Engle, Madeleine. *The Irrational Season.* New York: The Seabury Press, 1979.

――― *Walking on Water.* Wheaton, Illinois: Harold Shaw Publishers, 1980.

Lazarre, Jane. *The Mother Knot.* New York: McGraw Hill Book Co., 1976.

Leach, Penelope. *Babyhood.* New York: Alfred A. Knopf, 1983.

Lepp, Ignace. *Death and Its Mysteries.* Translated by Bernard Murchland. New York: The Macmillan Company, 1968.

Levine, Stephen. *Who Dies?* New York: Doubleday, 1982.

Lewis, C.S. *The Great Divorce.* New York: Macmillan Publishing Co., 1946.

Lynch-Fraser, Diane. *The Complete Postpartum Guide.* New York: Harper and Row, 1983.

Maslow, Abraham H. *Toward a Psychology of Being.* New York: D. Van Nostrand Co., Inc., 1962.

Maynard, Joyce. *Domestic Affairs.* New York: Times Books, 1987.

McBride, Angela Barron. *The Growth and Development of Mothers.* New York: Harper and Row, 1973.

Neale, Robert E. *In Praise of Play.* New York: Harper and Row, 1969.

Padovano, Anthony T. *Dawn Without Darkness.* New Jersey: Paulist Press, 1971.

Pearce, Joseph Chilton. *Magical Child.* New York: E.P. Dutton, 1977.

Peck, M. Scott. *The Road Less Traveled.* New York: Simon and Schuster, 1978.

Radl, Shirley. *How to Be a Mother and a Person Too.* New York: Rawson, Wade Publishers, 1979.

Rich, Adrienne. *Of Woman Born.* New York: W.W. Norton and Co., 1976.

Rilke, Rainer Maria. *Duino Elegies.* Translated by J.B. Leishman and Stephen Spender. New York: Norton, 1963.

Satir, Virginia. *Peoplemaking.* Palo Alto, California: Science and Behavior Books, Inc., 1972.

Scott-Maxwell, Florida. *The Measure of My Days.* New York: Alfred A. Knopf, 1968.

Spencer, Anita. *Mothers Are People Too.* Ramsey, New Jersey: Paulist Press, 1984.

Suzuki, Shunryu. *Zen Mind, Beginner's Mind.* New York: John Weatherhill, Inc., 1970.

Thomas, Lewis. *The Medusa and the Snail.* New York: The Viking Press, 1974.

Vanauken, Sheldon. *A Severe Mercy.* San Francisco: Harper and Row, 1977.

Walker, Alice. *In Search of Our Mother's Gardens.* San Diego: Harcourt Brace Jovanovich, 1983.

Ward, Theodora. *Men and Angels.* New York: The Viking Press, 1969.

Westerhoff, John. *Will Our Children Have Faith?* New York: The Seabury Press, 1983.

White, Burton L. *The First Three Years of Life.* rev. ed. New York: Prentice Hall Press, 1985.

Winnicott, D.W. "Mind and Its Relation to the Psyche-Soma." In *Collected Papers.* New York: Basic Books, 1958. Quoted by Judith Viorst in *Necessary Losses.* New York: Simon and Schuster, 1986.

Wordsworth, William. "Ode: Intimations of Immortality from Recollections of Early Childhood."